STORMING THE GATES

*How the Russian Revolution
Changed the World*

LIBERATION MEDIA

SAN FRANCISCO

Contributors

Brian Becker, Richard Becker, Jodi Dean, Gloria La Riva,
Alexandra Kollontai, Peta Lindsay, Candice Yanez

Editor

Jane Cutter

Staff

Meghann Adams, Peter Adams, Jon Britton, Sarah Carlson, Anne Gamboni,
Patricia Gorky, Erika Hidalgo, Saul Kanowitz, Susan Muysenburg,
Keith Pavlik, Michelle Schudel, Walter Smolarek

Liberation Media

2969 Mission Street #201
San Francisco, CA 94110
(415) 821-6171
books@LiberationMedia.org
www.LiberationMedia.org

Storming the Gates

STORMING THE GATES
How the Russian Revolution Changed the World

Preface

SOCIALISTS and communists around the world are taking the occasion of the 100th anniversary of the Russian Revolution to pay tribute to the first socialist revolution: to assess how it changed the world of 20th century politics; to continue a long-standing and unfinished process of evaluating the strengths, weaknesses and contradictions of the state born from the first successful workers' revolution.

The capitalist media and academia are also commenting on the Russian Revolution on this centennial. Unlike socialists and communists, however, their assessment is a self-serving caricature of reality.

The Russian Revolution took the state power on November 7, 1917 (new calendar). Although the ruling classes of the world tried to strangle this socialist baby in its crib, the Russian Revolution miraculously survived, but at great human cost. By 1920, after three years of imperialist invasions, civil war and famine, Russia and its peoples were nearly on their knees. During the next half century the Soviet Union became an industrial powerhouse. The Soviet Red Army was the decisive force in the defeat of Nazism. It was the principal protagonist of the United States in the so-called Cold War. In 1991 the Soviet Union imploded politically and went out of existence as an entity by January 1992.

This book is not a history of the Russian Revolution or comprehensive evaluation of its strengths and weaknesses.

With the exception of three newly-published articles, this is an anthology of previously published works by members of the Party for Socialism and Liberation, assembled to commemorate the 100th anniversary of the Russian Revolution. It has an introduction by Brian Becker, a chapter by Jodi Dean and a new prescient piece by Peta Lindsay on the Russian Revolution's impact on the struggle for Black

IV   STORMING THE GATES

liberation. The anthology features articles by PSL members on various aspects of the revolution and their lessons for today.

As stated in the introduction to this book, "It is a requirement of every socialist to have a position on the Soviet Union." In fact, it would be hard to take seriously a self-proclaimed socialist who had no position whatsoever on such an important matter.

Our attitude and approach towards the Soviet Union has always been a key defining aspect of the Party for Socialism and Liberation. We have taken an independent stance towards the Soviet Union — importantly combined with an unwavering defense of the USSR and its historic achievements against counterrevolution and imperialism.

This collection puts together in one place PSL's perspective on the Russian Revolution, an event which truly "shook the world." □

Introduction

The importance of the 100th anniversary of the Russian Revolution

BY BRIAN BECKER

IT is a requirement of every socialist to have a position on the Soviet Union. What was its class character? How could it accomplish so much? How could a country that was a latecomer to industrialization, and saddled by a largely backward peasant-based economy, tempestuously industrialize in the shortest possible time becoming the second largest economic and military power within a few decades, and then a few decades later come apart, politically implode, unravel and disappear?

Born out of two revolutions in 1917 and a bloody three-year civil war that followed, the rise and fall of the Union of Soviet Socialist Republics changed the course of world politics in the 20th century. Conversely, the absence of the Soviet Union as a counterweight to a U.S.-led imperialist world has shaped the first part of the 21st century as well.

The seizure of power by the Bolsheviks created a government whose foreign policy was unlike any other. Its initial pronouncements indicated just how different it was: It denounced imperialism, affirmed the rights of colonized peoples to throw off the shackles of foreign domination, and proclaimed that this revolution in "backward" Russia was nothing less than the first shot in a worldwide socialist revolution against the capitalist and imperialist ruling classes of the world.

The effect was immediate and electrifying. To the "global east" and "global south," young freedom fighters suddenly embraced communism and Bolshevism, and formed new communist parties to lead their struggles for national independence and self-determination.

In the "global west," the socialist movement split into two camps: communism on the one hand and social democracy on the other. Mass

v

communist parties took shape throughout the centers of advanced capitalism — from Europe to Japan and even the United States.

In the camp of the imperialist countries, the Bolshevik-led revolution created a panic of an unprecedented nature. Fourteen imperial armies invaded Russia to fight alongside reactionary "White" armies led by former czarist commanders and reactionaries. The first "Red Scare" was unleashed against leftists and against Black radicals throughout the United States. Thousands of leftists were arrested in the Palmer Raids in 1919-20, an operation led by 24-year old J. Edgar Hoover. Many socialist, anarchist and communist immigrants were summarily deported.

THE FIRST OF ITS KIND

The Russian Revolution was unique. It was the first time in world history that a non-property-owning working class seized political power and held on to it.

In the American Revolution and French Revolution of the 18th century, the transfer of political power, i.e., the seizure of state power, was from one group of private-property owners and exploiters to another.

Invasions, revolutions, coups, conspiracies and assassinations have, through the millennia, resulted in the violent seizure of political power by one group or another. In every instance, their political power was wielded on behalf of a group of property-owning exploiter classes.

The Russian Revolution was different. The power was seized by revolutionaries who proclaimed their adherence to socialism and communism. They insisted that their goal was the eradication of any private-property-owning ruling class. This was to be a revolution on behalf of those who owned no property but rather lived by the sale of their labor power. Ruling classes everywhere understood the implications of this contagion spreading.

A REVOLUTION BASED ON TWO CLASSES

There was one very large caveat in this picture. Most of the people in Russia were not urban, proletarian workers who fed themselves and their families from income derived from wage labor.

Rather, 75 percent of the country's people were farmers — peasants who worked the land. While many were landless, millions

The brutal conditions for the Russian people during World War I were a catalyst for the 1917 Revolution.

owned small tracts of land; middle peasants owned a bit more land; and the kulaks, a relatively affluent farming strata, largely dominated the political and cultural life of rural Russia.

The Russian Revolution of 1917 was the consequence of an alliance between the wage-owning, propertyless, urban working class and the large peasant mass that saw in the revolution, not the eradication of their private property, but rather their ability to seize the property that they worked on but which belonged to the large landed estates and landlords.

It was czarist Russia's catastrophic involvement in World War I that drove hungry, land-starved peasants into violent, revolutionary action in 1917 against the landed estates of the Russian aristocracy at the very same time the urban working class came under the leadership of Lenin and the Bolsheviks.

INDUSTRIALIZATION, COLLECTIVIZATION AND A NEW WORLD WAR

The capitalist class in the urban areas was dispossessed of its property. Later, in the 1930s, the Soviet government launched a massive collectivization and industrialization campaign that radically changed property relations in the vast Russian peasant countryside.

The socialist revolution of Nov. 7, 1917 was a nearly bloodless affair. The collectivization of the 1930s was nothing short of a civil war. The fighting and the ensuing famine that lasted from 1929 to 1935 took a heavy toll on people, livestock and agricultural production.

Industrialization in the main centers of capitalism was a process that had taken more than a century. But the leaders of the Soviet Union recognized and acted on the urgent need to rapidly transform the country from a rural, small-scale, private, peasant and farm economy to an industrial power capable of competing in all areas with the capitalist West.

The tempestuous all-out pace of collectivization and industrialization was a point of huge debate and created widespread turmoil inside the country and within the Communist Party of the Soviet Union. The 1930s were a wrenching decade. Tens of millions of peasants poured into the cities and took their place in the grueling work of the industrial factory. The small land plots of millions of peasants were aggregated into larger collective farms with the goal of introducing large-scale farming techniques, mechanization, the replacement of farm animals with tractors, the use of industrial fertilizers and

Young women arrive at the mines of Gorlovka
in eastern Ukraine under the Komsomol Appeal, 1930.

PHOTO: RIA NOVOSTI ARCHIVE, IMAGE #21733

other modern farming methods that were impossible as long as the land was divided into tiny, privately-owned plots.

On June 22, 1941, the largest part of the German war machine invaded the Soviet Union. It was a surprise attack that ended the German-Soviet non-aggression agreement. This was a pivotal moment in the twentieth century. Eighty percent of Germany's military divisions swept east into the Soviet Union. German military units crashed through the Soviet military lines and encircled hundreds of thousands of troops, while the German Luftwaffe destroyed a significant part of the Soviet air force on the ground. By the end of the war 27 million people in the Soviet Union had died. To understand the staggering character of this toll, one need only compare it to the casualties of the United States (419,000) and Britain (450,000).

Hitler, like the other imperialist politicians in the West, including Roosevelt and Churchill, fully underestimated both the industrial and thus the military capacity of the Soviet Union, not to mention the heroic determination and resolve of the Soviet people to resist. It was the Soviet Union that smashed Nazism. It was the westward Soviet counter-offensive that began in 1944 and liberated the peoples of Eastern and central Europe from the scourge of fascism, liberated the concentration camps, and led to the collapse of the Hitler regime. In fact, the United States and the British only opened up the Western Front of the war against Germany in 1944 when it became evident that the Soviet counter-offensive would otherwise leave the Red Army as the sole force to liberate all of Western Europe.

Despite the hardships and cruelties that accompanied the mad dash to industrialization in the 1930s, it is beyond dispute that the creation of Soviet industry was indispensable in the military struggle to defeat the German war machine. This industrial drive was carried out by the state. The factories were public property. The "profits" from state enterprises were used to plan and fund additional production according to state planning, not hoarded by a fabulously wealthy class of capitalist owners.

The Soviet leadership had always dealt with the question of how to technologically "keep up" with the West. This was both a national security and a political imperative, as socialism was prized as being a higher stage of human development.

Indeed, having nationalized and socialized all the basic sectors of the economy, utilizing a centrally planned economy and iron discipline, the government achieved remarkable economic feats. The economy was rapidly industrialized, which allowed the country to defeat the Nazi invaders. After the war, it was then rebuilt from the ashes with remarkable speed and by the late 1950s and early 1960s had even begun to match and surpass the West's most advanced scientific achievements.

THE COLD WAR: TWO SOCIAL SYSTEMS IN GLOBAL CONFLICT

Although the goal of the Soviet leadership in the aftermath of the defeat of fascism was to peacefully coexist with their wartime allies, Britain and the United States, the imperialist governments treated the Soviet Union and other socialist governments as mortal enemies.

One must understand the genesis of the Cold War. The sheer magnitude of the violence of World War II led to the collapse of the existing world imperialist/colonial systems. National liberation movements and socialist revolutions swept Asia. Anti-colonial movements in the Middle East and Africa were on the march. Communist movements were getting stronger throughout the "global south" and "global east." The communist parties in France, Italy and Greece were the dominant political organizations in society, and the Soviet Red Army remained in the countries that it had liberated from fascism in much of Eastern Europe.

The relationship of forces between the Soviet Union and world imperialism shifted dramatically in the decade immediately following World War II. The USSR was no longer the only socialist government. In China, communists came to power in 1949 following an epic 27-year long armed struggle. Communists took the power in the northern half of Korea and in the northern half of Vietnam. If it had not been for the partition of the two countries as a post-war arrangement between the Soviet Union and the United States, all of Korea and Vietnam would have been under the control of communist forces led by Kim Il Sung and Ho Chi Minh, respectively.

The Soviet leadership made these concessions because they were hoping to come to a peaceful arrangement with the United States and Britain following the war. The Soviet goal was to avoid another war. But the intensifying confrontational position of U.S. and British imperialism in the face of the global sweep of revolutionary movements led to a full scale imperialist counter-attack. Some of the flash points of the global class struggle included the revolution in China in 1949 followed by the wars in Korea and Vietnam; the civil war in Greece; the Berlin crisis of 1948 and the constant covert war to overthrow the socialist governments in Europe for the next three decades; the CIA coups from Iran to Guatemala to the Congo to Indonesia; the U.S. and British invasion of Lebanon and Kuwait following Iraq's revolution in 1958; the Bay of Pigs invasion of Cuba and the subsequent blockade; Israel's seizure of the West Bank, Gaza, the Golan Heights and the Sinai in 1967; U.S. support for Portuguese fascism's war against the national liberation movements in Angola, Guinea Bissau and Mozambique; and U.S. support of the racist, apartheid system in South Africa.

WHAT MADE THE USSR VULNERABLE

Despite all of the international challenges and economic problems caused by perennial labor shortages, imbalances between town and country, overspending on the military, lack of access to global technologies and other extreme pressures imposed by the pace of economic growth, there remained within the Soviet leadership a high confidence in the socialist system.

There were three areas of particular vulnerability, however, that deeply affected the Soviet leadership and its overall confidence, especially as it transitioned to a new political grouping that came of age in the middle of the Cold War.

First, in the 1970s the Soviets lost their technological edge with the emergence of the high-tech revolution in computers and electronics centered in the Western capitalist countries and Japan. The Soviets were completely blockaded from importing new technology from the capitalist West.

Second, at the same time, the U.S. government took advantage of the political conflict between the Soviet Union and China, the two largest socialist countries, and played them off each other. The result was the United States and People's Republic of China entered into an anti-Soviet alliance. China was allowed to integrate into the world capitalist economy, thus achieving access to the latest technologies emanating from the imperialist-led countries in what was called the high-tech revolution.

Third, the socialist governments of Eastern Europe were inherently weak since they were not the by-product of authentic revolutions of the people, but rather the consequence of the Soviet Red Army's presence following the defeat of fascism. The decision by the USSR to proceed with the socialization of the countries of Eastern Europe came about later in the 1940s after it became clear that the United States and Britain were rejecting a path favored by the Soviet leadership which was to create "neutral" governments in the territories that bordered the USSR's western flank.

Thus, revolutions from the top in countries that had been dominated by fascism a few years earlier created an uncertain political situation. Right-wing political forces did not vanish, but they were not permitted to operate openly. The exception to this process in Eastern Europe, was Yugoslavia, where the communist-led partisan army, under the leadership of Tito, defeated German imperialism and proceeded to create a socialist government.

In the two decades following the close of World War II, and in the context of the sharpening global confrontation, the Soviet economy continued to grow steadily but with many problems. There were constant efforts to innovate. New economic reforms were proposed with the goal of overcoming contradictions and imbalances in a planned economy suffering from the effects of being isolated from trade and exchange with the leading centers of the industrialized world.

A constant theme by the 1960s was how to improve the production of consumer goods when the economic model and scarce resources continued to favor industry and the production of military goods. Big problems in agriculture were a regular theme of internal debates and political struggles. By the mid-1970s the Soviet economy began to slow. Its annual growth rate continued to be positive rather than negative (recession), but the rate of growth was clearly slowing and declining.

The economic situation continued to deteriorate during the 1980s. The notion sunk in that the country had decisively fallen behind and would be isolated from the huge leaps forward taking place around them in the capitalist countries. How the Soviet Union could keep up with the new developments in technology — in computers, electronics, automation — appeared not only as an economic issue but went straight to the existential questions of national security.

Moreover, the Soviet leadership looked enviously at China's sudden and dynamic economic growth. There was a strong sense that the People's Republic of China was gaining economically and technologically from its reintegration into the world capitalist economy while the Soviet Union's economy was experiencing stagnation. China had cast off its leftist, revolutionary orientation of the Mao era, entered into an anti-Soviet alliance with U.S. imperialism, allowed capitalist property relations to be partly restored and was thus benefiting from huge new foreign direct investment by the leading capitalist corporations from the West and Japan.

The 1980s witnessed a shocking internal crisis in the summits of the Communist Party of the Soviet Union. After numerous short-lived changes in the top leadership of the old guard of the Communist Party in the Soviet government in the first half of the 1980s, a new generation of leadership took the helm in 1985. Within six years the entire edifice of the political leadership broke apart. Hastily adopted economic reforms, instead of solving structural problems, drove the economy into the ground. Nascent bourgeois political, ideological and economic forces that had existed in the shadows emerged to vie for power and to privatize public property. Anti-communist ideologues took control of important media outlets. Throughout the governments of Eastern Europe, pro-capitalist elements seized leadership and helped bring down already-divided governments.

Inside the USSR a dynamic, counterrevolutionary thrust was met with passivity and confusion by what appeared to be an ossified political institution. The Communist Party was declared illegal in 1990 as counterrevolutionary Boris Yeltsin suddenly rose to power in Russia. By January 1992 the Soviet Union, a multinational state comprised of 15 republics, went out of existence. Each republic became independent.

A near counterrevolution also took place in China at about the same time. The Communist Party of China's policy of alliance with Western imperialism led to a major division within the Party as well as a grassroots pro-capitalist uprising among some privileged, nascent-bourgeois students. Deng Xiaoping and other leaders of the Chinese Communist Party thus moved to use the People's Liberation

XIV STORMING THE GATES

Army in June 1989 to clear the seven-week-long counterrevolutionary occupation of Tiananmen Square.

This decisive action, which was denounced by all the centers of imperialism and falsely caricatured as the "Tiananmen massacre," prevented China from going down the same road of counterrevolution which overthrew the USSR and the governments of Eastern Europe. Although Deng and his faction had inaugurated many of the pro-capitalist reforms in China that inadvertently birthed this new bourgeois student movement, the same CPC leadership was deeply connected to the original revolution. They had helped lead a protracted armed struggle. They were not about to stand by and watch while reactionaries and imperialism coordinated the endeavor to seize power from the CPC.

> *Fidel Castro said that the demise of the USSR was the greatest single defeat in the history of the working class.*

TWO COUNTERREVOLUTIONS: THE DEFEAT OF THE PARIS COMMUNE AND THE OVERTHROW OF SOVIET POWER

The collapse of the USSR — the ignominious overthrow of the second most powerful country in the world — was not the consequence of an invasion, a civil war, a military coup or a natural disaster. There were some street mobilizations but no long-lasting barricades, nor prolonged fighting in the streets. Unlike in China, the party split apart.

Fidel Castro said that the demise of the USSR was the greatest single defeat in the history of the working class.

That event was the biggest historic defeat for the worldwide working class not only because of its immediate political and economic impact. The character and form of the defeat had a particularly demoralizing and dissipating effect on the worldwide movement for socialism and communism.

The defeat of the Paris Commune in 1871 was also a grievous, historic defeat for the working class. The Commune was the first time that the working class had taken control of state power. Within a few months the Commune was crushed in a bloody massacre, but the Communards went down fighting. Tens of thousands died. Their heroism in defeat became a symbol of resistance and an inspiration for future Communards in Russia, China and everywhere.

The overthrow of Soviet socialism offered no such example of heroic fighting to defend the first workers state. The struggle between those who wanted to retain the system and those who wanted to restore capitalism and integrate the country into the world capitalist economy was largely played out in a confusing struggle between factions within the summits of the Communist Party of the Soviet Union. The working class in large measure remained passively on the sidelines watching, functioning as spectators while the "leaders" and the media, which had been captured by anti-communists, battled with each other.

The failure of the working class to intervene at this moment of crisis was a clear indicator of something wrong, but it was not that the people desired to privatize their workplaces and hand the economy over to billionaire oligarchs, as the capitalist media claimed. Confusion, passivity and inertness were widespread. The absence of widespread working-class resistance to the counterrevolution indicated the extent to which the early flame of independent political activism had been extinguished.

Over the decades the working class had watched on as the leaders in the CPSU made the political decisions. The Party was presented as the repository of political knowledge, its apparatus was "the" legacy of the revolution itself, its decisions were "correct" and thus its deliberations had, over time, come to supplant and then extinguish the independent working-class activism that had given the 1917 revolution its energy, emancipatory dynamism and heroic self-sacrifice. Those were the key to the revolution's survival during the first efforts at counterrevolution, when the young socialist country was targeted by the invasion of 14 imperialist armies fighting alongside other counterrevolutionary armies and militias.

THE DECISIVE ROLE OF LEADERSHIP

One need only look at the writings, debates, controversies and political struggles inside of Russia during the first ten years after the 1917 revolution to grasp how democratic, engaging and energizing the impact of the revolution was on the working class. Without a doubt the working class in Russia was the most politicized in the world.

The frankness and openness about the problems facing society, the government, the economy and the Party are evident in every one of Lenin's speeches and writings right up until he was completely debilitated by a devastating stroke in January 1923.

The leadership and the party talked openly about all the challenges, shortcomings and weaknesses of the process that they were pursuing in trying to build socialism in a country that was ravaged by hunger, famine, illiteracy, invasions, civil war and a complete economic blockade from the centers of the world economy.

This style of leadership had the effect of engaging and catalyzing the revolutionary energy of the working class so that they could overcome and survive what seemed to be overwhelming odds.

All socialists and communists who want to understand the unique leadership style of the Bolsheviks under the tutelage of Lenin need to read and study his speeches and reports to the 7th, 8th, 9th, 10th and 11th Congresses of the Russian Communist Party (Bolshevik) that took place between 1918-1922.

These interventions by Lenin demonstrated candor, frankness and openness about the problems and weaknesses of the communists and their government, combining an unshakable will and boundless determination with extreme flexibility in tactics. As with all revolutions, the leadership was young, vibrant and bold. In 1917 Lenin, 46, was known by his nickname "the old man." The average age of attendees at the Party Congress in 1917 was 29. In a survey taken a decade before the revolution, 60 percent of the Bolshevik membership was 24 years old or younger, and one of every five was a teenager.

Six decades later the composition of the party leadership was different in many ways. They were far older and importantly not at all connected as personal participants in the 1917 revolution. Rather they were politicians and managers who had ascended as a consequence of their administrative, political and managerial achievements, or through seniority with the party or state bureaucracy. The party was led in 1980 by Leonid Brezhnev, who was then severely ill and nearly incapacitated. He died in 1982 and was replaced by Yuri Andropov, a 68-year old member of the Politburo, who also died of illness within 15 months. In turn he was replaced as General Secretary by the 74-year old Konstantin Chernenko who died from illness eleven months later. The image of the Soviet leadership was transformed. With an aging and fragile leadership at the helm, the Soviet Union was also experiencing a significant slowdown from its earlier dynamic rates of economic growth. This situation was compounded by needless cultural restrictions, reinforcing the sense among young people of "stagnation" in the government.

When Mikhail Gorbachev became general secretary of the party in 1985, he represented the ascension of a new generation of leadership — now three generations removed from the actual 1917 revolution. He was trained as a lawyer. Tellingly, he was a favorite of the most right-wing anti-communist leaders in the camp of imperialism: Margaret Thatcher, the anti-union Conservative leader in Britain, and Ronald Reagan in the United States.

Thatcher beamingly announced "we can do business with him" when Gorbachev had visited Britain in 1984, the year before he was named general secretary. These were welcome words to those in the summits of authority in the Soviet Union. There was a strong sense among these leaders that the People's Republic of China was gaining economically and technologically from its reintegration into the world capitalist economy, while the Soviet Union's economy was experiencing stagnation. The United States had imposed an absolute blockade of technology on the USSR at the very moment when the high-tech revolution in computers and electronics was on the verge of reshaping and modernizing the means of production on a scale as grand as the industrial revolution.

U.S. president Reagan and USSR general secretary Gorbachev in Geneva, 1985

The Reagan administration had also launched a full-court press — an economic and political offensive reinforced by a huge increase in military spending — meant to further drag the Soviet Union into an arms race it could not afford or win.

Once in power Gorbachev announced a new doctrine labeled "universal human rights" to replace the Marxist theory of class struggle. Rich or poor, capitalist or wage worker, everyone would now be regarded as a human being each with a set of universal rights. Imperialist governments recognized that in this new formula the Soviet leadership was renouncing not only the class struggle in an abstract way but was diluting or softening any anti-imperialist position in its foreign policy. It was understood as a concession to capitalism — not a strengthening of socialism — and it only made their appetite for counterrevolution more voracious.

The Soviet Union was in obvious need of political and economic reforms. But the ones introduced by Gorbachev, "Glasnost," Russian for political openness, and "Perestroika," Russian for economic restructuring, set into motion a full scale and catastrophic unraveling of the economy, while simultaneously allowing open anti-communists with the backing of imperialism to take control of the mass media in the Soviet Union.

That unraveling dealt a major psychological blow to socialists and communists everywhere, even those who were severe critics of the Soviet leadership. A new slogan — or rather a slogan that had not been seen since 1917 — rippled through the press, academia, popular culture and classrooms across the globe: There is no alternative to capitalism. The vision of an egalitarian organization of society and its abundant resources was cast aside as a utopian dream. The ideological challenge to socialism was greater at the end of the 20th century than at the beginning of the century; instead of "socialism will never work" and the "workers cannot hold power," the new arguments went: "socialism was tried and failed."

THE RUSSIAN REVOLUTION AND
THE REVIVAL OF SOCIALISM TODAY

The Party for Socialism and Liberation was formed in 2004, thirteen years after the demise of the USSR. The world view and analysis of the Party for Socialism and Liberation grows out of a fundamental agreement with the conclusion that the overthrow of the Soviet Union was the greatest defeat ever suffered by the world working class. It has been our thesis, since we began the process of building, actually rebuilding a new communist party in the United States, that we were doing so in the context of what we described as an era of global counterrevolution. This era has been defined specifically by the overthrow and demise of the Soviet Union, which occurred through the vehicle of a largely peaceful counterrevolution.

The U.S. military actions against independent nationalist governments from Iraq to Libya to Syria, the establishment of AFRICOM by the Pentagon, the huge assault on basic social programs for working people in the capitalist countries, the ideological offensive that declared communism is dead — these are just some of the features of the era of global counterrevolution. If Venezuela had a Bolivarian Revolution in 1960, it would have been able to "go all the way" because it could have affixed itself to a world socialist system and resisted the punishing economic sanctions and economic warfare, not to mention military assault, with which it must contend.

When we decided to begin building the Party for Socialism and Liberation, we did so with an openly-expressed understanding of the unfavorable international climate created by the overthrow of the strongest and most advanced socialist state.

The era of counterrevolution will not end all at once. But capitalism and imperialism cannot dispense with the contradictions of its economic order by simply thumping its chest and proclaiming "We won the Cold War." Arrogant triumphalism and the proclamation of its own immortality ("the end of history") by a terminally ill-social system will not actually give it eternal life.

A quarter of a century following the overthrow of the Soviet state, socialism is now rising again as a mass political current. Socialist organizations are growing. Young people in particular, less infected by Cold War propaganda, are gravitating to socialist ideas as the alternative to capitalism, a system that produces savage brutality and exploitation on a daily basis, that pushes all workers and nations into a "race to the bottom" so as to appease banks and corporations. It is fitting that all this coincides with the centennial of the Russian Revolution, the event that established for all time that the working class could and would seize power and hold it through the mechanism of a people's revolution and the creation of a workers' state.

The ideologues of capitalism proclaimed and still insist that the demise of the Soviet Union meant the end of socialism and communism as an alternative to the system based on private property, profit and exploitation.

This is both ahistorical and wishful thinking. The ultimate collapse of the first socialist experiment will not save capitalism. The system's crises and contradictions, its foundational feature requiring human exploitation and the class division of the human family into oppressed and oppressor classes, means that the class struggle and thus the struggle for equality and socialism will continue to rage. From this perspective, it is the conviction of the Party for Socialism and Liberation that the Russian Revolution and the Soviet Union will not be remembered in history as the end of communism but rather its first real-life initiation, marking a heroic, pioneering effort — the lessons from which will be emblazoned on the banners and in the consciousness of all socialists and communists of future generations. ☐

STORMING
THE GATES
How the Russian Revolution
Changed the World

The October Revolution: workers take power

BY RICHARD BECKER

O N April 3, 1917, Lenin, Zinoviev and other leaders arrived in a sealed car on a train. The German government allowed them to return to Russia across Germany and through German-held territory because it hoped that they would take Russia out of the war and relieve the pressure on Germany — that was explicitly the German government's reason.

E. H. Carr, an English historian, wrote a tremendous 14-volume history of the Bolshevik Revolution. Here is how Carr describes the scene of Lenin's return:

> Alexandra Kollontai produced a bouquet which Lenin carried awkwardly; and the party proceeded to the former imperial waiting room. Here, Lenin was officially welcomed by Chkheidze, the president of the Petrograd soviet, who, in a few carefully chosen words, expressed his hopes for 'a closing of the ranks of democracy' in defense of 'our revolution.' Lenin, turning vaguely away from the official party towards the assembled crowds outside, addressed them as 'dear comrades, soldiers, sailors and workers,' greeted in their persons 'the victorious Russian revolution,' declared that the 'robber imperialist war' was the beginning of civil war all over Europe, and concluded:

> 'Any day, if not today or tomorrow, the crash of the whole of European imperialism may come. The Russian revolution, made by you, has begun it and opened a new epoch. Hail the worldwide socialist revolution.'

As Sukhanov notes, it was not a reply to Chkheidze. It did not even fit 'the context' of the Russian revolution as understood by all without exception who had witnessed it or taken part in it. Lenin had spoken; and his first words had been not of the bourgeois, but of the socialist, revolution.

On the square outside the station, there was a mass demonstration of Bolsheviks headed by an armored car carrying the banner of the party. Lenin, standing on the armored car, addressed the cheering crowds in similar terms and, later on the same evening, spoke for two hours to a party audience at party headquarters. The slowly mounting astonishment with which his words were received by the other party leaders was described by an eyewitness ten years later:

'It had been expected that Vladimir Illich would arrive and call to order the Russian bureau of the central committee and especially comrade Molotov, who occupied a particularly irreconcilable position in regards to the provisional government. As it turned out, however, it was Molotov who was nearest of all to Illich.'[1]

LENIN'S CALL FOR A REVOLUTIONARY STATE

Lenin's position was a surprise, a big surprise. He produced a document that is very famous, "The April Theses," which basically asked and answered the question: What should the position of the Bolshevik Party be from this point forward? And he put forth this position: first, the war is a predatory imperialist war on Russia's part and it will be so as long there is this provisional government, a bourgeois government. It is not a revolutionary government. And as long as there is a capitalist government, because of the inseparable connection between capitalism and imperialism, and capitalism and imperialist war, this is an imperialist government and we regard it as such. Lenin said that the Bolsheviks could justify continuing a war only if the power was in the hands of workers and peasants; in other words, if it is a completely different kind of state. To step this up,

V. I. Lenin, 1919

Lenin called for fraternization and more connection between the soldiers of the different armies.

Secondly, Lenin said that they were passing from one stage
to the second stage of the revolution; passing from the first stage,
"which owing to the insufficient class-consciousness and organization of the proletariat, placed power in the hands of the bourgeoisie,
to the second stage, which must place power in the hands of the proletariat and the poorer section of the peasants." He argued, "Russia is
now the freest country in the world" of all the warring countries. This
was true. Russia was much freer than the United States, which at the
time was supposed to be the bastion of democracy in terms of what
people could do, what they could say and how they could organize.
And he said that the importance of the party is heightened because
the large mass of proletarians had just awakened to political life in an
unprecedented way.

Third, Lenin said that the Bolsheviks do not support this provisional government at all. This was completely different from what
even most in his own party had been saying. "Exposure in place of
the impermissible, illusion-breeding 'demand' that this government,
a government of capitalists, should cease to be an imperialist government."[2] Lenin acknowledged that the Bolsheviks were a minority,

a small minority and that they would have to act from that point of view. But he said that only the soviets of people's deputies could be a revolutionary government. That was the only possibility for a truly revolutionary government.

LESSONS FROM THE PARIS COMMUNE

Lenin called for a new type of state to replace the provisional government, and for the abolition of the police, the army and the bureaucracy. He said that the salaries of all officials should not exceed the average wage of workers, and that all officials who are elected should be recallable, not elected for two years or six months or four years or whatever, but always recallable by those who have elected them. This directly came out of the experience of the Paris Commune.

Lenin called for the nationalization of all the land; for the confiscation of big estates; and for setting up model farms. This idea is quite interesting in that model farms had never existed before. It was not just breaking up the old landed estates and dispersing the land, he said, but having model farms that the poorest peasants and agricultural laborers could run with support from the state. This was really the idea of collective farms or state farms.

A barricade in the Paris Commune, after it had been captured by the bourgeois army.

Lenin called for the nationalization of all the banks and consolidation into one bank. He said that workers have to bring all production and all distribution of products under the control of the soviets. He called for a change in the name of the party from the Russian Social Democratic Labor Party to the Communist Party. He called for the creation of a new International.

Now, this is a very wide-ranging program for someone who has just arrived. But above all, Lenin said, that they could not do it right at that time. He recognized that the Bolsheviks were in no position to call for the overthrow of the provisional government because they were not strong enough. But, Lenin thought, the whole orientation of the party should be the idea of all power to the soviets and making the soviets the government.

Two days after arrival, when Lenin took his ideas to the first party meeting he attended, the meeting of the Petrograd committee of the party, the vote was 13 to 2 against him. Only Alexandra Kollontai, a leading woman member of the Bolshevik Party, and Lenin voted in favor of his position. But Lenin eventually won over the party. He wrote: "There cannot be two powers in the state. Dual power is transitional. The provisional government is the government of the bourgeoisie. The soviets are the emerging dictatorship of the proletariat and the peasantry."[3] He emphasized that the provisional government represented the dictatorship of the bourgeoisie.

E. H. Carr wrote that on April 14, at the Petrograd conference, all the members of the party came together. And then, 10 days later, on April 24, when the Bolsheviks were able to hold an all-Russian conference of the party, there was a lot of opposition. At the beginning of both meetings, Lenin was in the minority. But by the end, his position won out strongly. "How did this happen?" historian Carr asks. And Carr answers, "The proceedings again demonstrate Lenin's immense power over the party, a power resting not on rhetoric, but on clear-headed and incisive arguments conveying an irresistible impression of a unique mastery of the situation."

In other words, Lenin won them over politically. This was not some kind of a cult experience. Lenin explained politically what was going on in a way that, it has to be said, no one else could. This raises a very interesting question, which has been discussed a lot, about the role of individuals in history. And Lenin's role has probably been the greatest subject of that discussion.

ALL-RUSSIAN CONGRESS OF SOVIETS

In May and June there were conferences, conferences and conferences. This was a revolutionary period. In June, there was the first All-Russian Congress of Soviets. It was a serious discussion. It lasted three weeks. There were 822 delegates. The Socialist Revolutionaries had 285, the Mensheviks 248 and the Bolsheviks 105. So, only about 12 percent of the delegates were Bolsheviks. But historically it is widely acknowledged that the most dramatic moment of this conference was when Tsereteli, who was the Menshevik minister of telegraph and post office, got up and made a speech and said: "At the present there is no political party which would say, give the power to our hands. Go away, we will take your place," referring to the coalition government. "There is no such party in Russia."

From his seat in the audience, Lenin shouted out, "There is." This is considered one of the turning points, because afterward Lenin got up and spoke about why the Bolsheviks were prepared to do that. A couple of months later, in a pamphlet called "Can the Bolsheviks Retain State Power?" Lenin went back to this incident. Carr calls this incident a "declaration of war" by the Bolsheviks on the provisional government. In recalling this, Lenin said: "I still maintain that a political party would have no right to exist, would be unworthy of the name of party, would be a nonentity in any sense, if it refused to take power when opportunity offers." Of course, opportunity did not really offer yet, but Lenin said that they were willing to take state power.

In the middle of June, Trotsky and a group of about 4,000 joined the Bolshevik Party. Kerensky, now the foreign minister in the provisional government and supposedly a socialist, announced plans to step up the war. Up until this point, there was not much happening in terms of Russia's war effort. But Kerensky announced, "In keeping with our treaty obligations, we will send the army into battle against the Germans." This caused a great deal of discontent in the country. A few days later, there was a demonstration called "Long Live the Soviets." It was called by all the soviets, in which the Mensheviks and the SRs were still the majority. But 90 percent of the banners in the demonstration were Bolshevik banners, with Bolshevik slogans.

THE JULY DAYS

On July 1, the provisional government launched a military offensive and the Russian army was sent into battle again. The army got smashed, with a huge number of casualties. Word quickly came back from the front, causing a huge uproar. The news of the new offensive triggered demonstrations by the workers in Petrograd, even before word of the results of the battle had reached people. In mass demonstrations, half a million workers came out, many of them armed and coming out for the soviets. It was on the verge of becoming an insurrection. The Bolsheviks felt, and correctly so, that the workers were not ready for this demonstration; they were not yet ready for an insurrection. But since the workers, the most militant workers, were going to the streets, the Bolsheviks decided that they had to go with them to the demonstrations.

After two days, the government brought in loyal elements of the army and, for the first time, opened fire on the workers. The Bolsheviks knew that if the workers demonstrated for a third day, there would be a slaughter. They were able to prevent the demonstration from happening. It was a setback for the revolution. Until July of 1917, everything had been moving forward, seemingly in one direction. The most

Petrograd Soviet meeting during the July days.

important thing, however, was that there was not a massacre of the most revolutionary elements.

The Bolsheviks were again driven underground. Trotsky and others were arrested. Lenin was hidden by workers in a remote working-class suburb of Petrograd. He would not emerge until the time of the October revolution. Pravda, the Bolshevik newspaper, was suppressed. But despite this, support for the Bolsheviks now began to increase. The Mensheviks and the SRs had not participated in this big demonstration of the most militant workers and their support began to go down. And the war was going on again.

It was still a down period. The lowest point was when a reactionary general named Kornilov, with the knowledge of some of the leaders of the provisional government, launched an attack. Kornilov gathered a reactionary army to attack Petrograd, the seat of the revolution, to try to smash the revolution. Others in the coalition government went to the Bolsheviks, as much as they hated to do so, to ask for help. They knew of the Bolsheviks' growing support among the most militant workers. In other words, they needed help from those who would really fight.

BOLSHEVIKS BECOME THE MAJORITY

Later, Lenin described this rescue as being similar to the way "a rope saves a hanging man" from hitting the ground. The Bolsheviks organized the Red Guards, detachments of workers who went out to confront Kornilov's forces. But there was never any shooting. When the Red Guards went out, Kornilov's forces ran. They just fled. So now, the Bolsheviks' standing and prestige soared. For the first time, in September, the Bolsheviks became the majority of those elected as deputies for the Petrograd, Moscow and other soviets. Trotsky was elected president of the Petrograd soviet — the most important soviet and the head of the whole revolution.

Lenin, who was still in hiding, called for the party to begin preparing for insurrection and to organize for the seizure of power. Developments had now created a power vacuum. The provisional government had lost credibility. The masses of people were disillusioned with the provisional government. They were sick of the war; they were sick of hunger; they were sick of being sick, and epidemics brought about by poverty, hunger and the war.

At the front, hundreds of thousands of soldiers were voting with their feet. They were deserting the army. They were either going to the cities to join the revolution or going home to the countryside, where many of them became agents of revolutionary change among the peasantry — this was to become a very important element. In the countryside, the number of seizures of big estates — plantations and latifundia, huge feudal estates with labor in a state of virtual servitude — doubled every month, for four months.

BOLSHEVIK POLICY IN THE COUNTRYSIDE

The Bolsheviks were relatively weak in the countryside among the peasantry. They had always been in the cities; they spent most of their existence underground and going out into the country had been hard for them. They were mainly a workers' party, but the peasants made up a huge majority of the population. The Socialist Revolutionaries were the main party in the countryside. The relationship between the peasants (farmers and agricultural workers) in the country and the workers in the cities was a key issue.

Based on a longstanding analysis, the Bolsheviks distinguished between the rich peasants, called "kulaks" in Russian, the middle peasants, the poor peasants and agricultural laborers. The kulaks owned large plots of land; they employed and exploited labor. The middle peasants owned land and basically had enough to live on. The poor peasants, were the majority of the population in the countryside. They lived on plots of land inherited from feudalism that were too small to yield enough food to sustain a family. They lived in destitution, were constantly going under, with their children starving and themselves starving to death.

Agricultural laborers were a growing sector in the countryside. They were poor peasants who had lost their land altogether and were really proletarians in the countryside. The Bolsheviks distinguished between these different layers and their strategy was to fight the kulaks, neutralize the middle strata, and win over the poor peasants and agricultural laborers.

Even though they were not a peasant party, the Bolsheviks were the only ones, from the beginning of the revolution that openly supported the peasants' seizing the big estates without compensation. Even the Socialist Revolutionaries took a position against the land seizures, stating that they would have to wait until there was a constituent assembly that could draw up the proper legislation and assure the land owners of how much they would be compensated. The Bolshevik stated that it was the right of the poor peasants to take the land and the big estates. But the SR leadership, while claiming to represent all the peasants, really represented the interests of the better off layers — the capitalist farmers and aspiring capitalist farmers.

The Bolsheviks' policy on land seizure caused the SR party to split. The left wing of the SRs, which was more political, more leftist and more based in the poorer peasantry, split from the SRs, and eventually, came together with the Bolsheviks for a period of time and formed a government after the October Revolution.

Lenin understood the question of the peasantry partly from his own personal experiences. He grew up in an agricultural area and as a youth he interacted with peasants to understand their situation. Around 1890, when Lenin was about 20 years old, he met somebody with whom he had a major discussion, arguing over what life was

In czarist Russia, peasants had no modern tools and worked endless hours.

like in the countryside. Before Lenin left for the university to attend law school, he talked this person into going out and surveying 200 peasant families and writing him about it.

Farmers are small capitalists or petit bourgeois. Since they own their means of production, their consciousness tends to take them in a capitalist direction. Lenin understood, through his experience and studies, that the small and poor peasants, as well as the agricultural laborers, had no hope under capitalism. They could only be crushed, exploited and forced to lose their land. This was the Bolsheviks' main orientation toward them.

As mentioned earlier, as a way of getting out of this life of 19-hour work days and abject poverty, Lenin called for setting up model farms. At the same time though, being realistic, he supported the breakup of the big plantations and the division of the land among the peasants who demanded it. If the revolution was to succeed in such a peasant-dominated country, there had to be an alliance between the workers and the poor peasants. Lenin's line was to show that the future for the small peasants was with the workers and with socialism. That was the only course that offered the peasants hope.

In 1917, Lenin wrote, "for the past 20 years, there has run through the whole political history of Russia, like a red thread, the question of whether the working class is to lead the peasants forward to socialism, or whether the liberal bourgeoisie is to drag them back into a compromise with capitalism."[4]

CAN THE BOLSHEVIKS RETAIN STATE POWER?

On October 1, 1917, Lenin finished the pamphlet titled "Can the Bolsheviks Retain State Power?" Now, that is a very interesting title for a pamphlet written when the Bolsheviks have not seized state power yet. This was written about 25 days before the insurrection took place. But Lenin was confident that they would.

In the pamphlet, Lenin wrote that "all of the trends are agreed, from the liberal capitalists to the Mensheviks, that the Bolsheviks will either never dare take over full state power alone, or, if they do that, and do take power, they will not be able to retain it, even for the shortest while." Lenin discussed some of the reasons for this perception. They said that the proletariat was too isolated from other classes, and from the real life forces of democracy.

They said that the proletariat would not be able to lay hold of the state apparatus, that it would not be able to set the state apparatus in motion, that it was impractical for the proletariat to do so, and so on. Lenin wrote:

> In addition to that we have a "magic way" to enlarge our state apparatus tenfold at once, at one stroke, a way which no capitalist state ever possessed or could possess. This magic way is to draw the working people, to draw the poor, into the daily work of state administration.
>
> To explain how easy it will be to employ this magic way and how faultlessly it will operate, let us take the simplest and most striking example possible.
>
> The state is to forcibly evict a certain family from a flat and move another in. This often happens in the capitalist state, and it will also happen in our proletarian or socialist state.
>
> The capitalist state evicts a working-class family which has lost its breadwinner and cannot pay the rent. The bailiff appears with police, or militia, a whole squad of them. To effect an eviction in a working-class district, a whole detachment of Cossacks is required. Why? Because the bailiff and the militiaman refuse to go without a very strong military guard. They know that the scene of an eviction arouses such fury among the neighbors, among thousands and thousands of people who have been driven to the verge of desperation, arouses such hatred towards the capitalists and the capitalist state, that the bailiff and the squad of militiamen run the risk of being torn to pieces at any minute.
>
> Large military forces are required, several regiments must be brought into a big city, and the troops must come from some distant, outlying region so that the soldiers will not be familiar with the life of the urban poor, so that the soldiers will not be "infected" with socialism.

The proletarian state has to forcibly move a very poor family into a rich man's flat. Let us suppose that our squad of workers' militia is fifteen strong: two sailors, two soldiers, two class-conscious workers (of whom, let us suppose, only one is a member of our Party, or a sympathizer), one intellectual, and eight from the poor working people, of whom at least five must be women, domestic servants, unskilled laborers, and so forth. The squad arrives at the rich man's flat, inspects it and finds that it consists of five rooms occupied by two men and two women – 'You must squeeze up a bit into two rooms this winter, citizens, and prepare two rooms for two families now living in cellars. Until the time when, with the aid of engineers (you are an engineer, aren't you?), we have built good dwellings for everybody, you will have to squeeze up a little. Your telephone will serve ten families.

This will save a hundred hours of work wasted on shopping, and so forth. Now in your family there are two unemployed persons who can perform light work: a citizen fifty-five years of age and a citizen fourteen years of age. They will be on duty for three hours a day supervising the proper distribution of provisions for ten families and keeping the necessary account of this. The student citizen in our squad will now write out this slate order in two copies and you will be kind enough to give us a signed declaration that you will faithfully carry it out.'

This, in my opinion, shows, by means of striking examples, how the distinction between the old bourgeois and the new socialist state apparatus and state administration could be illustrated.

We are not utopians. We know that an unskilled laborer or a cook cannot immediately get on with the job of state administration. In this we agree with the Cadets, with Breshkovskaya, and with Tsereteli. We differ, however, from these citizens in that we demand an immediate break with the prejudiced view that only the rich, or officials chosen from rich families, are capable of administering the state, of performing the ordinary, everyday work of administration. We demand that training in the work of state administration be conducted by class-conscious workers and soldiers and that this training be begun at once, i.e., that a beginning be made at once in training all the working people, all the poor, for this work.

This is a fascinating approach. Lenin is addressing one of the objections to the Bolsheviks taking state power: that they will not be able to administer the state because they do not have enough people. He is giving an idea of how the Bolsheviks can build up the state. But it is a very different idea of what the state is. The squad of 15 people is now part of the state. It is also interesting what Lenin writes about the exact makeup of this militia:

> We have not yet seen, however, the strength of resistance of the proletarians and poor peasants, for this strength will become fully apparent only when power is in the hands of the proletariat, when tens of millions of people who have been crushed by want and capitalist slavery see from experience and feel that state power has passed into the hands of the oppressed classes, that the state is helping the poor to fight the landowners and capitalists, is breaking their resistance. Only then shall we see what untapped forces of resistance to the capitalists are latent among the people; only then will what Engels called "latent socialism" manifest itself. Only then, for every ten thousand overt and concealed enemies of working-class rule, manifesting themselves actively or by passive resistance, there will arise a million new fighters who have been politically dormant, suffering in the torments of poverty and despair, having ceased to believe that they are human, that they have the right to live, that they too can be served by the entire might of the modern centralized state, that their contingents of the proletarian militia can,

with the fullest confidence, also be called upon to take a direct, immediate, daily part in state administration.

These lines were written a month before the October Revolution took place. Lenin's view is based, to a very large degree, on something that Lenin was committed to: that the poorest and most oppressed of the working class have this tremendous role to play in the future. What we see in this pamphlet is an expression of confidence in the proletariat. It shows not only Lenin's tactical brilliance but also his thoroughly revolutionary view.

In early October, there was still vacillation and opposition within the Bolshevik leadership over the question of seizing power.

This orientation also explains why the Bolshevik majority in the soviets, when it came to pass, looked so different from when the Mensheviks and the Socialist Revolutionaries had been the dominant force — this is also described by Trotsky in one of the chapters of "The Russian Revolution."

Another argument against the seizure of power — and this was the view of almost everyone on the left, including the Bolsheviks — was that a socialist revolution could not be sustained in Russia without revolution taking place in the more economically developed countries of Europe. But Lenin and Trotsky believed that the Russian revolution could be the first, and could spark others. Whereas the more passive view, the Menshevik view, was that they just had to wait. Unfortunately, none of the other revolutions that followed, in Hungary, Germany, Slovakia and elsewhere, succeeded.

In early October, there was still vacillation and opposition within the Bolshevik leadership over the question of seizing power. The moderate socialists, the Mensheviks, and even their more left-wing elements, were totally opposed to it and were speaking out very openly against it. It is important to point out that this struggle between the Mensheviks and the Bolsheviks had gone on for 14 years, since 1903. The Mensheviks constantly wanted to push the liberal bourgeoisie forward as the leadership, to have them speak on behalf of the movement. From the very time of the split in the Russia Social Democratic Labour Party, in 1903, the Mensheviks had said that it was the liberal bourgeoisie that must lead the next stage of the revolution into the bourgeois capitalist phase in Russia.

In the 1905 revolution, the Mensheviks had the same view. When the war came, they ended up supporting the liberal bourgeoisie, which was for the war. And in 1917, in the February Revolution, all the way through, the Mensheviks kept saying that the bourgeoisie had to lead because this was the bourgeois phase of the revolution.

> The Bolsheviks proceeded with preparations for insurrection and the seizure of power.

We see the same thing in the left in the United States too, where moderate socialists say, "Oh, we don't want to have revolutionaries speak at rallies. Let's just get the big names because we want to have broader actions." But not to have the revolutionary line presented is to take a position of constantly relying on the liberal bourgeoisie or the radical middle-class elements.

The Bolsheviks proceeded with preparations for insurrection and the seizure of power. Lenin, who was in hiding but in constant communication, was getting frustrated because the process was moving too slowly. Lenin understood that if power was not seized, the revolutionary crisis would pass and the possibility of taking power would disappear.

DEMOCRATIC CENTRALISM

The bourgeoisie was seeking to regain its footing, to reassemble its forces in alliance with the monarchists and all kinds of reactionaries. The bourgeois forces had suffered a blow, but they had not been totally defeated. They were going to come back. The Bolsheviks organized the Military Revolutionary Committee to carry out the practical preparations.

But in the days right before the insurrection, two leaders of the party, Zinoviev and Kamenev, came out against the insurrection, not only within the party but publicly. They spoke out in other newspapers and this compromised and threatened the insurrection. It jeopardized the revolution. This violated the Bolshevik organizational principle of democratic centralism; that is the party has to have internal discussions, but when it has made its decision it has to act in a unitary way. This is what democratic centralism in a revolutionary party is

Storming the Winter Palace in Petrograd, 1917.

made for in the long run: the revolution. But nothing shows more clearly than a revolutionary situation that not adhering to democratic centralism threatens even the possibility of a revolution. For example, if half the party says,   "Well, no, we've made a decision, but we're not into that so we're not going to do it; and, moreover, we're going to denounce it, in public, in the bourgeois press, before the revolution happens," the task of a revolutionary seizure of power becomes even more difficult.

When Zinoviev and Kamenev spoke out in this way, they were expelled, even though they had been long-time leaders from the very beginning of the Bolshevik Party. Later, after the Bolshevik Revolution, they were readmitted to the Bolshevik Party after they acknowledged their mistake. They criticized themselves for what they had done. Zinoviev became the head of the Communist International and Kamenev and Zinoviev became leading figures in the socialist governments that followed.

On Oct. 25 and 26, the insurrection, the seizure of power, took place. The revolution took place in Petrograd, Moscow and other cities. In Petrograd, the capital, the takeover was virtually bloodless. No more

than a couple of people were killed. It was done with great efficiency
and with tremendous support from the working class. They seized
government buildings, the armories, the telephone and telegraph, the
railway stations and the centers of communication and distribution.

In Moscow, there was more fighting. There was a battle with
the military cadets, but the revolution spread very quickly. The following is a proclamation that was read on that day, October 25, in
the Petrograd Soviet:

> Comrades, the workers' and peasants' revolution,
> about the necessity of which the Bolsheviks have always
> spoken, has been accomplished.
>
> What is the significance of this workers' and peas-
> ants' revolution? Its significance is, first of all, that we
> shall have a Soviet government, our own organ of power,
> in which the bourgeoisie will have no share whatsoever.
> The repressed masses will themselves create a power. The
> old state apparatus will be shattered to its foundations
> and a new administrative apparatus set up in the form of
> the Soviet organizations.
>
> From now on, a new phase in the history of Russia
> begins, and this, the third Russian revolution, should in
> the end lead to the victory of socialism.
>
> One of our urgent tasks is to put an immediate end
> to the war. It is clear to everyone that in order to end this
> war, which is closely bound up with the present capitalist
> system, capital itself must be fought.
>
> We shall be helped in this by the world working-class
> movement, which is already beginning to develop in Italy,
> Britain and Germany.
>
> The proposal we make to international democracy
> for a just and immediate peace will everywhere awaken an
> ardent response among the international proletarian masses.

All the secret treaties must be immediately published in order to strengthen the confidence of the proletariat.

Within Russia, a huge section of the peasantry has said that they have played long enough with the capitalists and will now march with the workers. A single decree putting an end to landed proprietorship will win us the confidence of the peasants. The peasants will understand that the salvation of the peasantry lies only in an alliance with the workers. We shall institute genuine workers' control over production.

We have now learned to make a concerted effort. The revolution that has just been accomplished is evidence of this. We possess the strength of mass organization, which will overcome everything and lead the proletariat to the world revolution.

We must now set about building a proletarian socialist state in Russia. Long live the world socialist revolution![5]

Now the key question was: "Can the Bolsheviks retain state power?" Having taken power and trying to spread this power through the country, would they be able to hold onto it? Despite everyone predicting this was going to be shorter than 72 days that the Paris Commune lasted, the Bolsheviks held on. Against unbelievable odds, against all of their enemies and opponents around the world, the Bolsheviks showed the world that they could hold state power. For the first time in history, not only did the oppressed masses fight and die for a cause, not only did they fight and die for justice, but they took power in their own name. They held onto it despite invasion by 14 imperialist armies and the mobilization of the whole of anti-communist Russia — from the czarists to eventually the Mensheviks, who fought bitterly against them.

The left Socialist Revolutionaries, who split away from their party, were with the Bolsheviks for a period of time, but by August of the next year one of them attempted to assassinate Lenin. He shot Lenin in the head, which led to his early death in 1924. Some of them eventually joined the Bolshevik Party. From all of the parties on the left, the more revolutionary elements joined the Bolsheviks. But as parties, they continued in alliance with the bourgeoisie, from the civil war to interventions that followed.

The Russian revolution could not have succeeded without the support it received from the workers in other countries, despite the fact that revolutions were not successful in those countries. This support included uprisings against the countries that were intervening in the civil war – like the rebellion in the French navy. A lot of armies that were sent into Russia had rebellions and mutinies by the troops. Also there were demonstrations of workers all over the world that supported the Russian Revolution.

The Russian revolution, in turn, inspired millions around the world, not just in capitalist countries but in the colonized world as well. One of the greatest things that the Russian revolution showed was that imperialism could be defeated, that the imperialists were not invincible. From that point of view, it is justified to say that up to that point the Russian Revolution was the greatest event in human history.

It also showed that only the kind of party that Lenin had built, a vanguard party, could lead a socialist revolution. What happened in Russia between 1903 and 1917 was a great testing ground. For all the different currents of the socialist movement, of the supposedly revolutionary movement, of the Marxist movement, only one emerged and was able to lead a revolution to victory — and that was the Bolshevik Party, a type of party that was different from all others. □

The early years of the Russian Revolution

BY RICHARD BECKER

THE Russian Revolution marked the beginning of a new period in human history. It was the first time that the oppressed were able to come to power — to take it and hold onto it. It truly had a transforming effect on the world.

First, let us review a quote that is good to keep in mind when analyzing the Russian Revolution. It is from Karl Marx's pamphlet: "The Eighteenth Brumaire of Louis Bonaparte." Marx wrote: "People make their own history, but they do not make it just as they please. They do not make it under circumstances chosen by themselves, but under circumstances directly encountered, given and transmitted from the past." This is an important idea. People make history, but they cannot just decide to do whatever they want. They have to do it in the context of the objective conditions they face. In dealing with the Russian Revolution, or in dealing with any of the countries that have attempted to build socialism, too often people start with questions like: Why could they not just do whatever they wanted to do? Why could they not just plunge ahead and accomplish everything that they might have wanted to, or everything that someone else may have thought they should?

Of all events, the Russian Revolution inspired the greatest hope among working people of the world, among those who aspired to build a society based on justice and equality. This included not only the working class, but also those from oppressed nationalities, everyone who was looking for a way out of the situation at the time. This is at a time when what later became known as the Third World in Asia and Africa was virtually all directly colonized. Latin America was mostly in a semi-colonial dominated position. The newly born Russian Revolution also inspired progressive intellectuals and artists

— many of whom went there even before it was the Soviet Union, which was formed in December 1922.

THE WORLD OF 1917

If we look at the conditions of the world in 1917, we can see why the Russian Revolution was such an inspiration. Imperialist powers dominated the world. In Asia, Africa and Latin America, people were dominated and exploited. Workers in capitalist countries were very oppressed, poor, and for the most part downtrodden. Racism and white supremacy reigned, along with the oppression of women. It seemed as if this was to be the permanent condition of the world and it was hard to see how there could be a way out of it. This situation existed even in the most "democratic" of countries, as the United States was referred to at that time.

In addition, 1914 had seen the beginning of the most destructive war in history. By the time the Russian Revolution took place in 1917, millions had been killed in trench warfare and tens of millions more were maimed, made homeless and starving. For the overwhelming majority of humanity, it looked like a world descending into hell. But a tiny section of the world's population went on living in indescribable luxury.

It was in this world that the workers and peasants of the Russian Empire rose up. They toppled one of the oldest monarchies and, under the leadership of the Bolshevik Party, not only overthrew the monarchy but set about on a course to rebuild, on a socialist and egalitarian basis, this giant country — with 11 time zones, compared to four for the United States. Not only that, but the Russian revolutionaries openly declared that their intention was to help the workers and the oppressed peoples of the entire world to liberate themselves from capitalism and imperialism.

To merely say that the Russian Revolution had a big impact is an understatement. The Russian Revolution was like a light shining out in a very dim and dark world. And it drew toward itself all of the progressive humanity who heard about it. Of course, given the level of communications at the time, not everyone could hear and it took a while for the word to get out. But the Russian Revolution quickly became a magnet and transformed the world politically.

The big question in world politics became: "Are you for the Soviet Union or are you against it?" As soon as the Russian Revolution took place, it surpassed other issues in importance. It became the fundamental question in 1917, and remained so until the time of the collapse of the Soviet Union in 1991. And it continues to be a big question today.

OBSTACLES FACED BY SOVIET RUSSIA

The question this chapter addresses is not why the USSR was overthrown in 1991, the subject of a whole other discussion, but how did it survive until 1921? Whether it would survive or not was a very big question. For the same reasons that the Russian Revolution attracted the enthusiastic support of the world's oppressed, it also drew the bitter hostility of the world's oppressors. The landlords, aristocrats and bourgeois elements from all over the world set out to kill this young revolution before it could grow and consolidate itself.

> *The landlords, aristocrats and bourgeois elements from all over the world set out to kill this young revolution before it could grow and consolidate itself.*

The Bolsheviks and Soviet Russia faced odds and obstacles that appeared to be too great to overcome. In the previous part of this Milestone series, we discussed the pamphlet "Can the Bolsheviks Retain State Power?" That pamphlet was written by Lenin three weeks before the revolution took place. He raised the question at the time because he was certain that the Bolsheviks were going to take state power. In early 1918, two months after the revolution, the answer to the question: "Can the Bolsheviks retain state power?" would have appeared to be no. It did not seem possible because there were too many forces arrayed against them.

But, in that period, in Petrograd, Moscow and elsewhere, there was revolutionary optimism. Among the Bolsheviks, the optimism was based not just on hope but on a firm conviction that the Russian Revolution was just the beginning — the first episode of an unfolding world revolution, which would soon spread, first to the countries of central and Western Europe and then beyond. They all believed that without new revolutions in the more economically developed countries the Russian Revolution would not be able to survive. All the Bolshevik leaders shared this belief — including Lenin, Trotsky, Zinoviev, Stalin and the rest — regardless of what their future positions were to be.

THE THREE GREAT TASKS OF THE REVOLUTION

Sam Marcy wrote a pamphlet in the late 1970s called: "Eurocommunism: New Form of Reformism." At the beginning, Marcy discusses the great tasks that the Russian Revolution faced.

The new, infant workers' state, the Union of Soviet Socialist Republics, had thrust upon it three Herculean tasks utterly unprecedented in the entire history of class struggle.

It had the duty and obligation to reorganize on a revolutionary basis the left wing of the social democratic movement, put it on a communist basis, and lay the foundation of a new and revolutionary international. Lenin and the Bolsheviks were thus obliged from the start not only to give revolutionary leadership at home but, in a way, to become the general staff of the world revolution, which seemed visible on the horizon, especially in Western Europe and later in the East, China.

Its second task, no less urgent and ultimately connected with it, was for the new workers' state to defend itself against the most barbaric assaults by the united front of the imperialists, from Vladivostok to Murmansk.

And thirdly, it had to begin to lay socialist economic foundations and raise the living standards of the workers and peasants, who had passed through a most horrible period of destruction, civil war and famine.

These three interlocking tasks: defending the country, which involved building a new military because the old one was gone; building a new economy based on socialism, which had never been done before; and reorganizing the world movement; any of which would be a monumental achievement, had to be done all at the same time, immediately after taking power.

DEFENSE

To get an idea of the problem of defense, we need to remember that the Bolsheviks had taken a position opposed to the imperialist war. They wanted to end it. But the war did not end; it was still going on after the revolution, and it was to continue for a year after the revolution took place. In the war, Russia, France, England and Italy — now joined by the United States that had just entered — were lined up on one side. On the other side, the main powers were Germany and the Austro-Hungarian Empire, whose troops occupied much of the western part of Russia.

What could the Bolsheviks do about this situation? The people were exhausted. The war was a large part of the reason why the revolution occurred. They wanted to end it but they still faced this aggressive imperialist enemy. So the Bolsheviks entered into negotiations with Germany, hoping that, with the growing unrest all over Europe, the workers, particularly in Germany, would rise up and force the German government to make peace and withdraw its troops. The Bolsheviks were really counting on this at first.

In the first days of the Russian Revolution, Trotsky was the People's Commissar of Foreign Affairs. Interestingly, his attitude was that the Bolsheviks would not need to carry on foreign affairs. He thought that the Bolsheviks would just publish all the secret treaties dividing up the world between the imperialists, make some arrangements to have an exchange of prisoners and that would be it. But as it turned out, that was not a realistic approach because the revolutions elsewhere did not happen. A cease-fire was agreed upon in December 1917 between Germany and Soviet Russia.

The Soviet negotiators tried to stall and to issue appeals to the workers in Germany to rise up. But most of the appeals were blocked. When the revolution in Germany did not happen, the Bolsheviks had to enter into real negotiations. There were three options.

One was to call for a revolutionary war against the occupying forces, but they no longer had much of a military force — only a few regiments left from the old czarist army. They had actively worked

Soviet WWI poster 'The enemy wants to capture Moscow,
the heart of Soviet Russia; the enemy must be destroyed;
forward, comrades!'

ARTIST: VLADIMIR IVANOVICH FIDMAN

to break up that army to make the revolution possible. But now they were facing the German army, the most powerful in the world.

Another option was to sign a treaty, which could only be a bad choice.

For a while, Trotsky tried a third option, a policy of "we are out of the war but we are not signing the treaty." The Germans would not accept this and launched a new offensive in February 1918.

By March, the Bolsheviks were faced with the fact that the German military was aiming to drive right into Petrograd and Moscow and destroy the revolution altogether. So the Bolsheviks signed the infamous Treaty of Brest-Litovsk. They decided, and this was Lenin's view, to accept the treaty and hope that things would be different later and that the terms would be changed. Accepting the treaty meant the Bolsheviks had to surrender a huge amount of territory to the German Empire. This included all of the Ukraine — the breadbasket of the old Russian Empire — as well as Estonia, Latvia, Lithuania and Byelorussia, known as White Russia at the time. In the south, the Turkish Empire, the Ottomans, took over Armenia and other areas.

Signing the treaty, however, did not solve the Bolsheviks' military problems. By the time it was signed, the White armies — extremely brutal armies led by various czarist military officers — had launched a campaign called "White Terror." The White armies would go into villages where there was sympathy for the Bolsheviks and the revolution and slaughter everyone.

At this point, in 1918, Russia was reduced to a small size. We know how huge czarist Russia had been and how large Soviet Russia was to be. It was being attacked from all sides. Beginning in April and May of 1918, while World War I was still going on, the Japanese Empire landed troops in the Far East, at Vladivostok, up to then under control by the revolution. The United States came in and then more and more forces invaded until there were 14 different imperialist countries involved.

It was an incredibly difficult situation. It appeared that the Bolsheviks could not survive and would be gone in a matter of weeks. Without an army, the Bolsheviks put all their attention toward defense. Transferred from foreign affairs after the treaty of Brest-Litovsk, Trotsky was put in charge of forming what was to be called the Red Army.

So that was one huge task the Bolsheviks faced: defending the revolution.

THE ECONOMY

The second task had to do with the economy and rebuilding it. Before the revolution, in the "April Theses", Lenin had laid out his position about the revolution. To summarize, Lenin said that the working class needed to control the economy but that it should not be socialized immediately. The socializing of the economy, Lenin said, had to be done over a period of time and that it would have to be developed because otherwise it would be too disruptive and break things up. But, as it turned out, there was not really a choice. For the most part, the capitalist owners fled. They took everything that they could with them, including their capital, their money. It was similar to what happened after the revolution in Nicaragua in the late 1970s, where much of the capitalist class just took everything they could out of the country, and the ones who stayed tried to subvert the economy.

And this was combined — later in other revolutionary countries like Cuba and Nicaragua — with a blockade, totally cutting off Russia from the world. In that period, nobody would sell revolutionary Russia anything. In all of 1919, Russia was almost totally isolated from the world. The isolation was so complete that they could hardly even get a newspaper from Germany. There were no goods to trade and very little was being produced by the factories in Petrograd, Moscow and elsewhere.

The country was still 90 percent peasant in population. They had to have goods to trade with the peasants for food. The most elementary necessity of a workers' government is to feed the workers. If you cannot do that, you cannot do anything else — not to mention trying to improve conditions of the working people, which has to be the goal of a workers' revolution.

WAR COMMUNISM

Many of the peasants, particularly the wealthier ones called the kulaks, but also the middle peasants, were withholding their grain from the market. They held back vast amounts of grain and demanded higher prices than what the new workers' state could possibly pay. This led to the initiation of what came to be known as "war communism."

The party organized worker detachments in the cities, in the factories, that went into the countryside to get the grain. They requisitioned the food. In other words, they went and said: "We look at how much food there is in the village, how much food the individual farmers have (the wealthier farmers of course). This is how much we believe you need to survive. And since you will not trade with us, we have to take the rest of the food. We have to take it because otherwise the workers will starve and the revolution is gone." That was the policy of distributing scarce goods on the basis of need. The government did this without regard for, and in effect bypassing, the market.

The most important and most immediate need was that of the Red Army, which was fighting the invading forces. Food is really the most important ammunition that an army requires. An army cannot move, cannot do anything, without food.

War communism was idealized by some. There were those in the Bolshevik Party who said: "This is really a way in which we can go straight to communism. We can bypass socialism and go right to communism." But that was not its purpose, nor was this a realistic way of getting to communism. War communism was not based on a plan, with the Bolshevik leadership deciding that was how they could get to communism faster. It was based, as it was said, on the "iron necessity" of the time.

Another major point about the economy is that it all had to be geared for defense. The government had to produce the weapons, the uniforms, the boots, the shoes and the armored vehicles. They had to produce all of this internally. Nothing could be brought in from outside.

It is important to point out that a civil war is far different from a war between countries. Countries can decide to make an agreement between themselves. They can decide to move the border this way or that way and end the war in some form. But that is not possible in a civil war. A civil war is a war to the death between two opposing sides, because they cannot share power. The civil war in Russia was devastating.

So, after three years of World War I — the most devastating war in history — in which Russia had already lost millions of people, and under a blockade, the revolutionary government had to fight against the White Army as well as foreign intervention in a civil war. These circumstances led to a downward spiral in the economy. By 1920, industrial production in Russia was only 14 percent of what it had been in 1913! It is almost impossible for us to conceive of what that means. Effectively, six out of seven of everything we can think of, everything people need, was gone. During the Great Depression, at its worst, the U.S. decline in production was something in the neighborhood of 40 to 50 percent. In Russia, there was a decline of 86 percent. There was starvation and there were epidemics. It was such an extreme situation that by 1920 and 1921, there was the reappearance of cannibalism in some areas.

REORGANIZING THE WORLD WORKING-CLASS MOVEMENT

It is important to be honest about what really happened to understand what comes later for Russia and the Soviet Union. In early 1918, the Bolshevik Party had maybe a quarter of a million members. The conscious elements of the working class, other revolutionary elements, and peasants who had been in the army and politicized, numbered maybe two million.

There are objective conditions and subjective forces in a revolution. That is, the objective, material conditions that exist and have come into being, and the subjective forces being the politically conscious elements, and there is a relationship between the two. But when a revolution happens, that subjective force, the politically conscious population, becomes an objective condition as well. Without this particular objective condition, things could not have gone very far in the Russian Revolution.

Not only did the Bolsheviks have to deal with this war of annihilation against them on all fronts as well as the hunger and the economic collapse, but they also had to take on reorganizing the left wing of the working-class movement in the world. It was not a secondary task; it could not wait. The Bolsheviks could not wait because they regarded the extension of their revolution to other countries as an absolute necessity for their own survival. They were all completely dedicated to this. An indication of this is that shortly after the revolution, as soon as the war ended, Karl Radek, one of the leaders of the revolution, went to Germany and became an agent for revolution there. But he was quickly found out by the German government and held in solitary confinement for six months.

The Bolshevik leadership had just gone through this whole revolutionary process. But their internationalism was of such a character that Lenin, Trotsky and other leaders repeatedly said that they did not see the survival of the Russian Revolution, their own revolution, as their number one priority. They said that if they had a choice of being able to take some action enabling revolution in Germany, and by doing so costing them power in Russia, they would do it. The German revolution, from their point of view, would have had so much greater effect on the whole worldwide struggle of the working class. Of course, they were still prepared to fight to the death for the Russian Revolution. But they believed

Karl Radek

that a German revolution would have much greater strategic weight.

THE END OF WORLD WAR I

In November 1918, World War I came to an end. Something rarely talked about is why it ended. The Workers' and Soldiers' Councils were taking power in Germany. In parts of Germany, starting on Nov. 6, 1918, the councils started functioning as the supreme political authority, bringing about the end of World War I. The workers and soldiers could not take it anymore. It had been four years of this war and they had had it.

The politically conscious German working class rose up.

But at that time, there was no revolutionary party in Germany. Nevertheless, in Russia, this was considered the hoped-for beginning of the revolution in Europe. On Nov. 11, which became Armistice Day, now Veterans' Day, in the United States, the Soviet government declared the Brest-Litovsk Treaty void, although German troops remained in the occupied areas. Now a revolutionary situation existed in Germany. In many cities, there were soviet authorities, the workers' councils, an alternative power much as they had been in the Russian Revolution in the period between February and October of 1917.

Alongside the workers' councils was another source of power, the government. After the Kaiser (German emperor) was overthrown and the Weimer Republic established, that government was headed by the Social Democratic Party. This mass workers' party had been taken over by an opportunist, pro-capitalist faction that still claimed to be socialist. Its social base was a minority of the more privileged workers, who in turn constituted the base of a major part of the trade union leadership and the party's parliamentary fraction, which overwhelmingly had voted for war credits on August 4, 1914. These misleaders had emerged and begun to move to the right some years before on the basis of the rise of German imperialism and an extended period of relative prosperity.

The bourgeoisie of Germany, which had lost all its authority as a result of Germany's defeat in the war, had no choice but to turn to the Social Democratic Party and ask it to become the government. They remained as the government until Hitler took power in 1933. During that time, they acted, effectively, on behalf of the German capitalist class.

In 1919, there were revolutions in Hungary, which lasted a few months, and in Bavaria, a southern state of Germany, which lasted only a few weeks. Over the next three years, there were several attempts at revolutionary seizures of power in Germany. The revolutionary situations, mainly in defeated Germany and the Austro-Hungarian Empire, which was now breaking up into smaller states, were all defeated.

Why did the revolutions fail? In a revolutionary situation such as in Germany, there were soviets in many of the cities. However, there was not a party like the Bolshevik Party that could pull together all the forces of the working class. Lenin later characterized the malady of the "left-wing communists" as an "infantile disorder."

In short, a party had not been organized that could unite the class, coordinate the movement, knew how to move, to be able to maneuver against the bourgeoisie and to call for a revolutionary insurrection. These are the main reasons that revolutions after the war failed in Europe.

THE COMMUNIST INTERNATIONAL

In March of 1919, the Bolsheviks held the first convention of the Communist International, the Third International, in Moscow. That year was the height of isolation for Russia. The isolation was so complete that people died attempting to get to this convention. Only 55 delegates, representing 19 countries, were able to attend.

The Bolsheviks conceived of the Communist International as an international communist party in which there would be national detachments and the world staff of the revolution. Lenin said of the Communist International, years before there ever was a USSR, "It's the union of soviet socialist republics of the world." At this convention, the Bolsheviks made an appeal to the workers of all countries to come to the aid of the Soviet Republic that was under such tremendous duress and said: "if you don't come to our aid, we will certainly die." They added: "If you don't come to our aid, we at least can die on our feet, while you will be condemned to living as slaves."

English language version of
The Communist International,
published October, 1919

The task of the Communist International was to try, as quickly as possible, to propagate the principles and tactics that the Bolsheviks had experienced and learned between 1903 and 1917, to build new revolutionary and communist parties — not opportunist social-democratic but communist parties — all over the world. This was no small task. This was not as big a task as the economy or as big a task as the war. But it meant that they had to have, from a limited number of people capable of dealing with all these tremendous challenges, people who were informed and educated down to the tiniest details about every country. This was necessary because they were having discussions with people from those countries about how to build the political movement, how to build the communist movement in Germany, France, the United States, Indonesia, China, all over the world. They had to set up departments and bureaus for different countries and parts of the world. It was a huge undertaking in extremely difficult circumstances.

The failures of the revolutions of 1918 to 1921 gave capitalism a breathing space. The United States had now become the leading power in the world because it sat out most of World War I and had taken relatively light casualties. U.S. casualties in World War I were around 117,000, compared with 3 to 4 million for Russia and 6 to 7 million for Germany. The United States had come late into the war and played a role similar to that of England in wars between imperialist rivals — supply all sides with arms and food, make huge profits from it, wait to see which side is winning, and then join that side late in the war. By doing so, the United States had become the leading economic power in the world. And through methods such as the Dawes Plan, the United States began to funnel in money to stabilize Western Europe.

The revolutionary wave was blocked by its own lack of preparedness (due to the lack of Bolshevik-type parties), by the intervention of the United States, and the relative re-stabilization of the capitalist system.

By 1921, what seemed to have been a totally hopeless situation in Russia had changed. The hastily put together Red Army and workers' and peasant militias, had pushed back the White armies. Even in 1921, large parts of the Caucuses region and the northern part of Russia were still occupied by invading armies. But the Civil War was effectively over. The Russian Soviet Federated Socialist Republic, as it was known then, had regained much of the territory it had lost, out to the Pacific Ocean. It was impoverished but still standing.

HOW DID THE RUSSIAN REVOLUTION SURVIVE?

How was this possible? The leaders of the Bolshevik Party had thought: "If we do not have other revolutions, we cannot survive. We are the most backward capitalist country. Facing all that we face, it will not be possible for us to live unless there are other revolutions." The answer to this question is that, despite the defeat of revolutionary working-class attempts in capitalist countries, particularly in Europe, the international working class was supportive of and sympathetic to the Russian Revolution.

The failure of other revolutions left Russia — which became the USSR in 1923 — isolated as a socialist country. But the imperialists were held back from massive invasions. None of the imperialists sent in a million troops, or a half a million troops, or anything close to that. Had they been able to do that, given their economic and military advantages, they probably would have been able to crush the Russian Revolution by sheer weight of force.

Why were the imperialists not able to invade with a large number of forces? E.H. Carr's "The Bolshevik Revolution" states:

> In January 1919, when the allied statesmen, assembled in Paris for the peace conference, discussed the occupation of Russia by allied troops, the British prime minister bluntly assured his colleagues that "if we now proposed to send a thousand British troops to Russia for that purpose, the armies would mutiny," and that "if a military enterprise were started against the Bolsheviki, that would make England Bolshevist and there would be a Soviet in London.

Lloyd George was talking for effect, as was his manner. But his perceptive mind had correctly diagnosed the symptoms. Serious mutinies in the first months of 1919 in the French fleet and in French military units landed in Odessa and other Black Sea ports led to an enforced evacuation at the beginning of April. Of the troops of several nationalities under British command on the Archangel front, the director of the military operations of the War Office reported in March 1919 that the morale was "so low as to render them a prey to the very active and insidious Bolshevik propaganda which the enemy are carrying out with increasing energy and skill." The details were disclosed much later through official American reports. On March 1, 1919, a mutiny occurred among French troops ordered to go up to the line; several days earlier a British infantry company "refused to go to the front," and shortly afterwards an American company "refused for a time to return to duty at the front." It was in the light of such experience that the British government decided in March 1919 to evacuate north Russia, though the evacuation was not in fact completed until six months later.

Mutiny among the troops was matched by widespread disaffection in the industrial centers of Great Britain. At the time of the armistice, a report handed by the Foreign Office to the American embassy in London expressed the belief that "apart from certain centers, notably the Clyde and South Wales, Bolshevism as such is innocuous for the present." Nevertheless, no chances were taken: "A careful watch is being maintained for such Bolshevik propaganda as may reach this country from abroad, in order that it may be intercepted and destroyed, and the same measures are being taken wherever possible in respect to inflammatory literature secretly printed at home. Counter-propaganda is meanwhile being conducted through the unostentatious distribution of pamphlets designed to educate the people as to the true significance of Bolshevism, and appropriate articles appear in the Sunday papers customarily read by working men."

The first serious attempt to challenge public order by calling a general strike was made in Glasgow at the end of January 1919; and "Red Friday" was long remembered as the peak of the revolutionary movement on the Clyde. Political discontent was focused on the government's Russian policy by a meeting at the Albert Hall on Feb. 9, 1919, which launched a "Hands off Russia" campaign. At the founding congress of the Comintern a month later, the British delegate Fineberg spoke in a language that seemed to find support in facts: "The strike movement is spreading all over England and is affecting every branch of industry. In the army, discipline is much weakened, which in other countries was the first symptom of revolution."

"England may seem to you untouched," Lenin told a British correspondent at this time, "but the microbe is already there."

Meanwhile, hunger was rife in central Europe, and disorganization was everywhere; strikes and disorders had occurred even in peaceful neutral countries like Holland and Switzerland. On March 21, 1919, just a fortnight after the founding congress of Comintern had dispersed, a Soviet Republic was proclaimed in Budapest. On the next day, House in Paris confided his apprehensions to his diary: "Bolshevism is gaining ground everywhere. Hungary has just succumbed. We are sitting upon an open powder magazine and someday a spark may ignite it."

There was a serious discussion going on, particularly by the French, to say: "Let us just organize a big allied force and go in and get rid of this because we know this is our enemy, our class enemy, and we should destroy it." But although the working class was not able to achieve political power in the other countries, as Carr's book passage indicates, sentiment had developed strongly in support of the Russian Revolution. It was because of this that the imperialists had to take into account what would happen if they tried to take too vigorous a military action, particularly when all of these countries were just coming out of a world war where the populations were so sick of war. Would being ordered to go to war again, this time against fellow workers in Russia, be the last straw? Would it push things over the edge? Would the imperialist powers face what happened in Russia in their own countries? This would not have been a consideration had there not been demonstrations and strikes, including here in the United States. There was a general strike in Seattle that demanded no intervention in Russia.

The contradiction that the Soviet state faced when this revolutionary wave was not successful was the basis for the real contradiction in its policy. On the one hand, the leaders wanted to promote revolution, and on the other hand if the revolution did not happen fast enough, they had to deal with the other states because there is a system of states in the world. On the one hand they were supporting the revolutionary movements in various countries to overthrow the governments, and on the other hand, they were sitting down to talk to those same governments. And those governments knew this, which was to come back as a much bigger issue later.

Against seemingly impossible odds, the most important factor in the survival of the new Soviet state, Soviet Russia, was the revolutionary enthusiasm unleashed by the revolution itself. Through their participation, workers became, for the first time, the subjects and not the objects of history. As mentioned previously, the revolutionary energy released by the revolution is, in a much more positive way, similar to a thermonuclear explosion. If you look at uranium, there is no way to conceive of the tremendous amount of energy released when there is fusion. There is no way of calculating this factor in history, of what people are really able to do, of what is really possible, of the potential that lies within the oppressed classes. This made it possible to attain what appeared to be unattainable.

In the process of attaining it, though, many of the most dedicated workers, most of the communist workers, were killed. They died in the battles to save the Soviet Union. Literally millions gave everything so that the first workers' revolution could live. And it lived, but under very difficult conditions. Because it lived, communism became a world force. Also, for the first time, there developed an area in the world that was under the control of the workers, under the control of the oppressed — one-sixth of the world was now in their hands.

But by 1921, Russia was exhausted. The workers who now worked in the factories were new workers. This is something to think about to understand what happened in the next few years in the Soviet Union. There were no longer workers who had lived through the rich, educational, revolutionary experiences from the late 1890s, when the working class began to become a factor in Russia, up until 1917. Most of those workers were lost. They were either dead or if they had survived, they were now doing some job in the state. They had to. It was a workers' state and that is where the personnel had to come

Fighting during the Russian Civil War

from. So now the workers were new arrivals from the countryside who did not have this kind of political experience and consciousness.

At the same time, in 1921, since the economy was still completely blockaded — with all that means in a modern, interconnected world — reforms to revive the nearly dead economy had to be carried out. These reforms were called the "New Economic Policy." The reforms were somewhat similar to what Cuba has had to implement under the conditions of no longer having the Soviet Union or the Eastern bloc to trade with. These reforms allow some capitalist incentives while trying to keep the commanding heights of the economy under socialist and workers' control.

These two factors together have a lot of implications for what happened later: the tremendous decimation of the most revolutionary elements of the working class, combined with being forced to adopt certain capitalist-type initiatives and reforms in the economy to survive, at least for a time.

EFFECT ON THE WORLD MOVEMENT

The last thing to be mentioned is that the Russian Revolution and the Communist International, despite all the problems that they faced, had a dramatic effect on the world movement and its politics. In the capitalist countries, all over Europe, in the United States and in Japan, new parties were organized out of the old socialist parties. New communist parties took all the most left-wing, revolutionary elements, and others who were new to politics, and formed new communist parties.

What was even more dramatic is that until this time, communist and socialist organizations had been mainly confined to the capitalist countries, to the imperialist countries. Now, in the course of the formation of the Communist International, Lenin said that they should change the slogan of "Workers of the World Unite" to "Workers and Oppressed People of the World Unite." As one of their primary objectives, they set out to give aid to not just revolutionary movements in oppressor countries, but to the oppressed countries in their struggle against imperialism. It changed Marx's fundamental slogan of "Workers of the World Unite" to include the oppressed peoples of the world, oppressed by imperialism.

One way this was expressed was that the Soviet government, within a couple of years of the revolution, signed a new treaty with

China. China was broken up into pieces and under imperialist domination. In the treaty, the Soviet leadership declared that it renounced all concessions, all privileges and the right of extra-territoriality. After the Boxer Rebellion in the late 1890s, China had been forced to pay all of the occupying countries a yearly indemnity, including to czarist Russia. The Soviet government renounced that and said: "We are done with the indemnity. We renounce all of the privileges."

This was startling. No imperialist country had ever done this voluntarily, and none has done it since.

The Bolsheviks published the secret treaties the czar had entered into with other imperialist countries. One of those was the Sykes-Picot Treaty. The British had promised the Arab people living in the Ottoman Empire, which was part of the British enemy camp in World War I, "If you fight on our side against the Ottoman Turks, when the war is over you will have your own country." In 1915, at the same moment that the British were making this promise, they signed the Sykes-Picot Treaty, a secret treaty with France and Russia by which they agreed that after the war, England would get Palestine, Iraq, Jordan and Kuwait, and the French would get Syria and Lebanon. In 1920, the Soviet government published it, which led to rebellions all over the Arab world. The publication of the treaty showed that the Bolsheviks were disclaiming any of the interests that had been entailed in the czarist treaties.

All these actions drew the most left-wing nationalist rebellious elements all over the world toward the Russian Revolution and toward communism, who now saw that imperialism could be defeated. They saw that the misery which had existed in Russia before the revolution and all over the world was not inevitable. They saw that it did not have to be a tiny group in control and all the rest oppressed. There was a way out, and the Russian Revolution showed the way.

In 1920, the Indonesian Communist Party was formed. It was hard to get from Indonesia to Moscow, but someone did. In 1921, the Communist Party of China was formed. The Communist Party of France contributed directly to the formation of a communist party in Vietnam. Without the Vietnamese Communist Party, Vietnam would never have been able to defeat the United States. In 1922, a communist party was formed in Chile. Also in South Africa, and within a few years in Iraq and Cuba, communist parties were formed all over the world, where imperialism reigned. Now imperialism had to face something completely new. Now people all over the world had new hope. There is a story recounted by E.H. Carr. There was a communist presence in Baku, Azerbaijan, part of the Russian Empire. The majority of the people there were Islamic and they hated the domination of the Russian Empire as well as imperialism. Among the people of Baku, word began going around that Lenin was a messenger of Allah. Of course, that is not what Lenin would like to be known as. But this story is an indication of what the Russian Revolution meant, how its victory was communicated around the world and the tremendous impact it had. ☐

Why we continue to defend the Soviet Union

BY GLORIA LA RIVA

The following was a talk given Nov. 13-14, 2010, at the National Conference on Socialism sponsored by the Party for Socialism and Liberation.

THE Soviet Union went out of existence 19 years ago next month. Some progressive people argue that given the fact that nearly two decades have passed, the issue of the Union of Soviet Socialist Republics is now an irrelevancy. We think otherwise.

For one thing, the capitalist class and its well-paid intellectuals and pundits continue to argue that the fall of the Soviet Union means that socialism and communism are impossible. These ideas might have been nice dreams at one time they say, but socialism turned out to be a nightmare when it actually came into existence.

A stereotyped and negative image of the Soviet Union has been relentlessly fed to the people ever since the Russian Revolution, which took place 93 years ago this month. This manufactured image reflected the fear and hatred of the world bourgeoisie toward the first workers' state.

Unfortunately, a significant part of "the left," including some so-called socialist organizations, bought into the anti-communist stereotypes and pressures. To their everlasting disgrace, they cheered the demise of the Soviet Union and the other workers' states in Eastern Europe, proclaiming these counterrevolutions great victories for "workers' democracy."

Few of the actual workers in those countries, who saw their living standards and even life expectancies plummet in the years that followed, shared this sentiment. In fact, to this day public opinion polls show majorities of working people in the former Soviet Union,

East Germany, Romania, and other countries longing for the system that they lost.

The triumph of the Russian Revolution nearly a century ago was truly a historic world event. It was the first time in history that the working class was able to seize and hold power, and to reorganize the economy and society on a socialist basis. It proved that the oppressed, with their own leadership, their own party, could create a new reality.

CHALLENGES FACED BY REVOLUTION

The new Soviet government, led by the Bolshevik Party, was immediately confronted with several immense tasks — any one of which would have been daunting. First of all, they had to defend their new state against not only the internal counterrevolutionary armies — the White armies of the old landlords and capitalists — but also against the entire imperialist world. Fourteen imperialist armies invaded the new-born workers' state, including the United States. They sought, in the words of the infamous imperialist and racist Winston Churchill, to "strangle the Bolshevik baby in its crib."

Second, the new government had to reorganize the economy and meet the needs of an impoverished — and often starving — population. They had to do this under conditions of a total economic blockade imposed by the capitalist world.

Third, they had to reorganize the workers' movement internationally and build a new Communist International. This was not an optional task: None of the Bolshevik leaders — Lenin, Trotsky, Stalin and others believed that they would be able to succeed unless there were other revolutions in more industrially developed countries, particularly Germany. And the biggest obstacle to revolutionary success there was the lack of a Bolshevik-type party.

The fact that the Russian revolutionaries were able to hold onto power in the face of these momentous obstacles seems almost unbelievable. It is a testimony above all to the immense human potential of the working class, which is suppressed under capitalism and only allowed to fully flourish by a socialist revolution.

The years of war and deprivation took an enormous toll on the party and the working class as a whole, a toll that weakened the party and later led to problems.

But contrary to the bourgeois presentation of a failed economic system, the Soviet planned economic system — the first time in history there ever was a planned economy — showed the remarkable potential of socialism.

GAINS SHOWED POTENTIAL OF SOCIALISM

From being the least developed of the big European countries at the time of the revolution, 40 years later the Soviet Union was the second largest economy in the world, trailing only the United States. It was the most rapid economic development ever, by any country. This despite the fact that after barely a decade of initial rapid development in the 1930s, two-thirds of the industry and much of the agriculture was destroyed by the Nazi invasion beginning in 1941. And contrary to what we see on the History Channel, it was the Soviet Union that bore the brunt of the Nazi war machine and destroyed it — but at a cost of 27 million killed. The U.S. death toll in WWII was about 400,000 — a huge toll itself but about 1.5 percent of the Soviet death toll.

Before the revolution, much of the population went through life without ever seeing a doctor. In 1966, a leading U.S. medical journal wrote that "life expectancy doubling in the last 50 years. ...At present time, the Soviet Union graduates annually about as many physicians as there were in whole Russian Empire before the First World War. Of all the physicians in the world today, more than one in five is Soviet ... while only 1 person in 14 in the world today is a Soviet citizen."[1]

Not only that, but none of those doctors — three-quarters of whom were women — paid a kopek for their education, nor did anyone else in any field of work. Of course, they could not hope to become millionaires. It was a fundamentally different system than the one we live in, more like the one in Cuba today. Every person was guaranteed the right to a job, housing, health care, childcare and education, and also the right to vacations, pensions and culture.

The Soviet Union showed the superiority of a socialist, planned economy by eliminating unemployment — something no capitalist country has been able to achieve. The key to ending unemployment was doing away with the capitalist system and its built-in boom-and-bust cycle.

A woman working in the Pravda newspaper print shop, 1959.
Such a practice was rare in the West at the time.

In the wake of the destruction of WWII, vast industrial, infrastructure and housing projects were undertaken. The absence of capitalist competition between enterprises enabled very rapid scientific and engineering development.

Full equality for women was a basic principle of the Soviet state. Special measures were taken to ensure equal representation at various levels of the workforce, and discrimination on the basis of gender was constitutionally banned. Women received at least a year of paid maternity leave.

The Soviet Union was organized on the basis of the right to self-determination, meaning that each nationality had the right to control the institutions that shaped its destiny, and the promotion of hatred on the basis of nationality was outlawed. The more than 100 nationalities in the USSR were each entitled to literature, newspapers and education in their language. Scores of languages that were not previously written were alphabetized. For the historically oppressed nations and regions, vast industrial, infrastructure and housing projects . were undertaken to compensate for the legacy of underdevelopment.

In 1957 the Soviets launched Sputnik, the first satellite to orbit the Earth, a testament to socialist advancement and shock to the U.S. imperialists. Four years later the USSR sent the first person, Yuri Gagarin, into space.

In addition to its remarkable internal development, Soviet aid was vital to national liberation movements and newly independent states around the world. The victories of the Chinese, Korean, Vietnamese and other revolutions would have been much delayed or prevented without the Soviet Union. Without Soviet support, Cuba would have undoubtedly been invaded by the United States, and Soviet aid was vital to the Palestinians and many African revolutionary movements.

PROBLEMS FACED BY SOVIET STATE

Recounting just some of the achievements of the Soviet Union is important because they are almost never mentioned these days. The achievements listed above are all the more remarkable given the serious problems the Soviet state faced. These problems included:

- The forestalling of revolution in the advanced capitalist countries, which could have provided immense assistance to the USSR. Instead, all of the subsequent revolutions were in countries less developed than the Soviet Union and needed and received aid from the USSR.
- The imperialist military encirclement of the USSR. Under U.S. policy, the word "containment" really meant overthrow, regime change. After World War II, the United States never demobilized its armed forces and instead launched a massive nuclear and conventional weapons buildup. U.S. bases were set up all over the world to surround the socialist camp of the Soviet Union, Eastern Europe and China. For the U.S. capitalist ruling class, military spending — which by now amounts to over $40 trillion since WWII (in 2010 dollars) — is the most profitable sector of the economy. For the ruling class in the Soviet Union — the working class — military spending meant a huge drain from economic

projects to meet people's needs. The vast buildup in military spending under Reagan in the 1980s was meant to destroy the USSR. After a couple years of huge military spending, someone said to Reagan, "This will bankrupt us." His response was, "Yes, but the Soviets will go bankrupt first."

- The capitalist world and particularly the United States modified but never ended their sanctions and blocking or sabotaging of trade, particularly in advanced technology goods. This was especially problematic in the late 1970s and 80s with the revolutionizing of communications and other technologies, which caused the Soviet Union to begin falling back in relation to the leading capitalist economies of the United States, Germany and Japan. By the early 1980s the rate of growth had slowed to 2 percent.

- Internal problems, particularly bureaucratization, a long-term de-politicization of much of the working class, and separation between the Communist Party of the Soviet Union and the masses of workers and collective farmers.

In 1978 a revolution in Afghanistan brought a progressive government to power. The CIA reacted by carrying out its biggest operation to date in support of a counterrevolution, and the Soviet Union intervened militarily in support of the revolutionary government. This military pressure combined with ongoing economic pressure, resulted in a long-term division in the CPSU's leadership erupting into a full-scale split. The pro-capitalist, pro-imperialist faction led by Boris Yeltsin and Mikhail Gorbachev won out.

By the late 1980s, the Soviet Union was cutting back or eliminating support for national liberation movements and allied socialist states. In 1989, the Gorbachev leadership broke the alliance with the communist governments and militaries in Eastern Europe leading to capitalist counterrevolutions in Hungary, Czechoslovakia, Poland, Bulgaria, Romania and East Germany, and the disintegration of Yugoslavia. In 1991 this traitorous group dismantled the Soviet Union itself, leading to the restoration of capitalism in the 15 now-independent republics. We agree with the assessment of Cuban leader Fidel Castro: It represented the biggest setback in the history of the working class.

But it did not mean — as some capitalist commentators proclaimed — either "the end of history" or the end of the struggle for socialism. The evermore urgent need for socialism is not based on the existence of any particular state, but instead grows out of the contradictions of the capitalist system itself, problems that the system cannot overcome — problems that only socialism can solve.

What is most remarkable from an objective standpoint, is not that the Soviet Union fell in 1991, but that it survived through the unimaginable challenges it faced. We should also remember that it took the bourgeoisie, the capitalist class, five centuries from their rise as a class until capitalism became the dominant world system.

The Soviet Union should be studied for its incredible achievements as well as its problems and contradictions. It was a first attempt. By its existence for more than seven decades it proved once and for all that the working class can take power and reorganize society on a socialist basis. □

Lenin's 'April Theses'

The role of leadership in revolutionary struggle

BY NANCY MITCHELL

The article below was first published in Socialism and Liberation *magazine in April 2005.*

THE 1917 Russian Revolution was the first time in history that the working class seized and held power, organizing a workers' state in the interest of the vast majority of toilers rather than a rich minority elite. This great revolution actually came in two phases. The February Revolution swept away the czar (king) and the old feudal ruling class.

The October Revolution overthrew the capitalist class and put Russia on the road to building socialism.

V.I. Lenin wrote the "April Theses" at a decisive moment in the aftermath of the February Revolution. They were written to give political orientation to the Bolshevik Party, which led the working class in the socialist October Revolution. Lenin argued that the working class could not remain subordinate to the capitalist class. The working class needed a second, socialist revolution.

PRE-REVOLUTIONARY RUSSIA

Prior to the Russian Revolution, the vast majority of the population were poor peasants subsisting in the countryside. The land-owning nobility met peasant uprisings for land and food with brutal repression. Capitalist industry was developing rapidly in the cities, but Russia had not experienced a bourgeois-democratic revolution like the other European imperialist powers. All classes were denied basic democratic freedoms as the country remained in the clutches of czarist absolutism.

The country was still ruled by the extreme repression of the czar and the old feudal monarchy. The bourgeoisie — the capitalist class of factory owners and merchants — was growing, but was still politically very weak as a class.

World War I broke out in August 1914. It was the bloodiest, most destructive event the planet had ever seen. The great imperialist powers were at war in a scramble to re-divide the colonized territories around the world. Russia formed an alliance with the British and French ruling classes with the promise of securing domination of parts of the Middle East and Central Asia.

Although they were initially drawn into the war based on patriotism and "Russian pride," the war turned out to be a catastrophe for the people. By 1917, millions of Russian workers and peasants had died, and much of the country's resources were diverted to the war. This led to food shortages and widespread hunger in the cities. All the while, the big landowners and the growing capitalist class lived in extreme decadence.

BREAD, LAND AND PEACE

The February Revolution of 1917 began on International Women's Day with a strike by women workers in Petrograd. They had three simple demands: bread, land and peace. The conditions of the

International Women's Day, Petrograd 1917

war and the deprivation were causing such an acute crisis that the workers could not take it anymore and took to the streets.

Over a period of five days, the protests grew. As the workers gained confidence and militancy, the soldiers stationed in Petrograd, who had been ordered to suppress the demonstrations, joined them. After five days, they toppled the government and overthrew the czar.

In the immediate aftermath of the February Revolution, the workers and soldiers established Soviets. The Soviets first appeared on the historical stage in the 1905 Russian Revolution, which although defeated, served as a dress rehearsal for the events twelve years later. Soviets were elected councils, organized by the workers and soldiers in each military unit and factory. They were the seeds of workers' power.

'PRESSURE' OR 'OVERTHROW' THE CAPITALISTS?

Russia's workers and peasants were represented by three main parties, all of which identified themselves as socialist. The Bolsheviks and the Mensheviks represented two distinct wings of the Marxist working-class movement, while the Socialist Revolutionaries were a peasant-based populist party.

As the czar's government fell, the leading parties in the Soviets, the Mensheviks and the SRs, turned toward the representatives of the capitalist class to take power in Russia. They believed the country needed more time to develop capitalism before being ready for socialism.

The workers were armed, mobilized and capable of seizing power. But they were not sufficiently conscious and organized to realize it.

The leadership of the Mensheviks and the SRs formed a coalition with the capitalists in a Provisional Government. The capitalists in the Provisional Government consented to work with the Soviets, making promises and using leftist rhetoric to appease the workers — while agreeing to the demands of British and French capitalism that Russia not withdraw from the war.

The Bolshevik Party had been the only party in Russia that opposed the war from the outset. Other parties, even those that called themselves socialist, capitulated to the intense pro-war hysteria to support "defense of the fatherland."

The Bolshevik Party was severely punished for its anti-war position. Party leaders, including Lenin, were exiled or imprisoned, and the party was forced into a clandestine or underground existence. While many Bolshevik party members participated in the fighting of the February Revolution, the party was too organizationally weak and politically disoriented to strike an independent course from the other left parties.

The period directly following the February Revolution was a joyous time for the workers of Russia. The workers had closed the book on 400 years of czarism, and the heavy repression of the czar was lifted. There was an overwhelming sense of excitement and optimism about the new "democratic" revolution.

The leaderships of the left parties believed they could compromise with the capitalists and "pressure" them to take good positions on the issues of land reform, workers' rights and, most of all, ending the war. Even the Bolsheviks in Russia, largely cut off from their exiled leadership, initially took a position of "critical support" for the Provisional Government.

From his exile in Switzerland, Lenin was urging the other Bolshevik leaders not to collaborate with the capitalist class. He said the policy of "pressure" was delusional. "To urge that government to conclude a democratic peace is like preaching morality to brothel keepers," he wrote.[1]

THE 'APRIL THESES'

Lenin finally arrived back into the country on April 3, 1917. He brought an argument that was later called the "April Theses." The main tenets were:

The current situation in Russia is one of "dual power" between the capitalist class and the working class. Now the workers must continue the struggle to achieve a socialist revolution and overthrow the capitalists.

Despite the demands of the February Revolution, the Russian capitalists are continuing to wage an imperialist war. The position of the party must be for an end to the war and the defeat of its own capitalist class.

The party must take the position of "No Support for the Provisional Government," and must direct its efforts toward the coming socialist revolution. It should prepare to raise the slogan: "All Power to the Soviets!"

In a country that was celebrating its newfound freedoms and a working class that was enamored with its new government, Lenin's position was not very popular. In the first party meeting to discuss Lenin's thesis, it was outvoted 13 to 2. At party conferences later in April, Lenin continued to argue his points and by the end, his position won out strongly.

The immediate interests of the working class, over which they fought the February Revolution, were bread, land and peace. Lenin knew that the Russian capitalist class could not meet these simple demands.

Lenin analyzed Russian capitalist interests in their international context. The Russian capitalists were inextricably linked to British and French imperialism. If they had any hope of becoming stronger as a class, they would never abandon their imperialist allies in World War I. Russia's survival as a player in the imperialist arena depended on its securing colonized territory for exploitation.

The bourgeois-democratic Provisional Government could make many promises to the people, but Lenin insisted they would not pull out of the war. In addition, any steps toward land reform would have caused millions of peasant soldiers to desert the war front in order to come home and claim land. This was a reform the capitalists could not afford.

The majority of the workers supported the Provisional Government in April. But Lenin's "April Theses" were premised on one irrefutable conclusion: The bourgeois government would not be willing or able to withdraw from the war. The crisis of the continuing war would ultimately force the workers to take the only action that could resolve their demands — overthrowing the capitalist class and starting the socialist revolution. Lenin argued that the party should orient itself to help lead the working class to this end.

While the other socialist parties were collaborating with the capitalists and attempting to "pressure" them in a more left direction, the Bolsheviks began to organize for their overthrow.

In "The Bolshevik Revolution," historian E.H. Carr wrote of Lenin's ability to win over the Bolshevik Party to his political position, that it was a "power resting not on rhetoric, but on clear-headed and incisive argument conveying … a unique mastery of the situation." Lenin's clarity of vision was based not on clairvoyance but on his ability to analyze class interests and to anticipate the potential of the working class to take power.

The "April Theses" is an important example of the critical role of leadership in discerning the right direction in a revolutionary situation. In April 1917, the Bolsheviks were a small minority party, but Lenin's political reorientation rearmed the party and put it on a revolutionary footing.

In April, May and June, support for the Bolsheviks grew tremendously. By September, they had won the majority in the Soviets. And in October 1917, with the revolutionary leadership of the Bolsheviks, the workers and peasants of Russia accomplished the world's first successful socialist revolution. □

Socialism and the legacy of the Soviet Union

BY BRIAN BECKER

THE single biggest event that shaped global politics in the 20th century was the Russian Revolution of 1917, which gave birth to the Soviet Union. The first socialist government's existence was the pivot for world events in history's most turbulent and dynamic century. The destruction of the Soviet Union 74 years later in 1991 has been the dominant factor shaping global politics ever since.

Karl Marx and Frederick Engels wrote in "The Communist Manifesto in 1848, "A specter is haunting Europe — the specter of communism." However haunting the specter of communism may have appeared to the European bourgeoisie in the mid-1800s, it would seem mild compared to the undiluted hysteria directed by all the imperialist powers and old ruling classes against the actually-existing Soviet Union throughout the 20th century.

The victory of the Russian Revolution transformed the presentation of communism from an idea or an ideology into a living, breathing social and political experience. It was an attempt to consciously build a society based on the interests and needs of the working classes.

Communism's new identification with a state power was extremely positive for the world communist movement. The domestic programs, the radical reorganization of constitutional law and the revolutionary foreign policy of the new Soviet state spread the appeal of communism to nearly every corner of the globe. Millions of people were drawn into political life and the communist movement as the idea of workers' power took on flesh and bones.

In the colonized world, the Soviet message of self-determination and freedom drew the most advanced youth directly into newly founded communist parties. From China to Vietnam to South Africa, the banner of Soviet communism became synonymous not just with socialism but with the aspirations for national independence.

As the influence of communism spread throughout the 20th century to all corners of the world, every capitalist power brought to bear the weight of its media, politicians, universities and especially armies in a global struggle to counter Soviet influence.

The identification of communism with a state power expanded later to its political association with the governments in Eastern Europe, China, North Korea, Vietnam and Cuba, along with newly founded revolutionary governments in Africa that were also trying to take a socialist road. Communism became inseparably connected to what was known as the "socialist bloc" governments. As the first, largest and most powerful socialist power, the Soviet Union was identified as the anchor of this global camp.

POLITICS, IDEOLOGY AND STATE POWER

Conflating the historical ideology and perspective of communism with a government or a bloc of governments also created a tremendous disadvantage, in spite of the material advantages that came from possessing state power. Every setback, weakness, retreat, defect and deformation suffered by the Soviet Union was also identified as an inherent negative feature of communism.

That the socialist revolutions took place in poor countries instead of the rich imperialist countries gave the capitalist propaganda machine ready-made ammunition to argue against socialism. Anti-communist literature could point to the relative affluence of the imperialist countries and assert, "Socialism or communism is nothing but the equality of poverty for the people while 'officials' and 'bureaucrats' enjoy privileges based on their association with the ruling communist party."

This same anti-communist propaganda, spoon-fed to the people of the United States, obscured and falsified every real social and economic achievement made by the Soviet Union, China or Cuba. Nowhere was it mentioned that every Soviet worker had a legal right to a job, free health care and free child care. Rent was a small fraction of income. Every worker was guaranteed one month of paid vacation.

These social rights were maligned or hidden in the West. In every instance, the propaganda emphasized that the capitalist United States was rich and affluent, with ordinary workers having access to all sorts of goods and services that were not accessible in the Soviet Union.

When the Soviet Union was overthrown in 1991, capitalist propaganda highlighted one theme: The collapse of the Soviet Union meant that communism itself was now dead. The dream of poor and working people was vanquished forever. "The end of history" was the theme of a best seller in 1992 written by academic Francis Fukuyama. The essence of this argument was that capitalism and the rule by a class of billionaires of and over society was the natural order of things.

NO ANTI-COMMUNIST UPRISING

The Soviet Union was not overthrown by foreign military intervention. Nor was it brought down by an uprising of discontented workers as happened with the October 1917 revolution. In fact, nine months before its dissolution, 77 percent of the people in the Soviet Union voted to maintain the country in a referendum taken as part of the March 1991 election.

That result did not interest the pro-capitalist "democrats" in the least. In December 1991, the leaders began the process that would see the USSR dissolved within the next year.

It was leaders from within the summits of the Communist Party of the Soviet Union that led the offensive to destroy the Communist Party and dismantle the Soviet Union. This initiated the sale and looting of publicly owned factories, real estate, oil, gas and mining enterprises and collectively owned agricultural lands and farms.

The wealth of society — at least significant parts of it — was turned over to a new class of private capitalists who soon became notorious for their opulence, decadence and theft. The legal social status of the working class was diminished and the standard of living of almost all workers plummeted.

The loss of factory jobs and access to medical care coupled with the attendant social problems and demoralization led to disastrous consequences. For example, a March 11, 1998, article in the Journal of the American Medical Association reported a drop in life expectancy for Soviet males from 63.8 years in 1990 to 57.7 years in 1994. The population in Russia actually dropped by over 500,000 people in the first eight months of 2000 — the steepest drop ever during peacetime.

A woman dumpster diving in post-Soviet Russia, 2014.

All the while, U.S. propaganda proclaimed that democracy and freedom had come at last to Russia.

A REVOLUTION LIKE NO OTHER

The Russian Revolution marked the first time in human history that the working classes, those without property, took the reins of power and held them. All previous revolutions in human history had transferred social and political power from one class of elite property owners to another.

The great French Revolution of 1789-93, for instance, had destroyed the power of the monarchy, feudal lords, landed nobility and aristocracy. The working classes had been the vanguard fighters in that revolution. But that revolution led to the French bourgeoisie taking power. The feudal mechanisms of exploitation based on serfdom were uprooted and destroyed, but were replaced by a new system of exploitation based on wage labor or wage slavery.

The October 1917 insurrection was altogether different from earlier revolutions. The social aims of the revolution, led by workers and poor farmers or peasants, were explicit about their class content.

Earlier revolutions masked their class character with broad slogans of freedom and equality "for all." The Russian Revolution, by contrast, explicitly proclaimed that eliminating all exploitation of the laboring classes was its principal objective on the road to achieving a society without classes. Operating under the Marxist conception that society was divided into antagonistic classes driven by mutual and irreconcilable differences, the explicit goal of the revolution was to achieve the political and social supremacy of the working classes over their former exploiters.

The banal slogan of "liberty and justice for all" was considered a mask concealing the true picture that the rich and privileged owners of private property had dominated society.

A WORKERS' CONSTITUTION

The victory of the Russian Revolution was based on the soviets — workers' councils that were the basic fighting organizations of the Russian workers. After the revolution, the soviets became the basic units of government. The first constitution adopted by the Congress of Soviets on July 10, 1918, set out the "fundamental goal" as "suppressing all human exploitation, abolishing forever the division of society into classes, ruthlessly suppressing all exploiters, bringing about the social-ist organization of society and the triumph of socialism in all countries."[1]

Soviet Constitution

None of the victorious revolutionary bourgeois governments from earlier epochs, even in their most revolutionary phases, would have thought of declaring this "fundamental goal" in their constitutions.

"As a first step toward the complete transfer of factories, works, shops, mines, railways and other means of production and of transport to the ownership of the workers' and peasants' Soviet Republic and to insure the supremacy of the laboring masses over the exploiters, the Congress ratifies the Soviet law on workers control of industry," reads another key provision in the constitution.[2]

Anticipating that the resistance of the overthrown exploiters would be greater following the revolution and that they would be aided by the imperialist governments of the world, the constitution declared that,

"In order to secure the supremacy of the laboring masses and to guard against any possibility of the restoration of the power of the exploiters, the Congress declares the arming of the laboring population."[3]

This clause might have seemed to be written by people with a crystal ball. Within months after the 1918 Constitution was adopted, the country was plunged into a bloody civil war pitting class against class. Fourteen imperialist armies, including the United States, invaded Russia between 1918 and 1920. Three million people died.

And yet, to the amazement of all, the new workers' state survived the onslaught.

PROBLEMS OF SOCIALIST DEVELOPMENT

A huge part of the politicized and consciously communist working class of Russia died as volunteers fighting for the new social order, however. By the close of the civil war, the cities were decimated by hunger and disease. The factories were without raw materials. The urban proletariat started to return to the countryside in search of food.

The economy had contracted by nearly 90 percent compared to the 1914 pre-World War I level. In order to resume production, Lenin and the Russian communists retreated in 1921 and allowed the return of capitalism and capitalists — but under the "supervision" of the Soviet state. The New Economic Policy was presented as an emergency step away from the communists' goals — to bend so as not to break. While it did stimulate production in both the countryside and the cities, it also led to a re-polarization of social classes, especially in the countryside.

It was not until 1928, when the economy was getting back on its feet, that the Soviet government resumed the push toward rapid socialization in the factories and the countryside.

In spite of these difficulties — all amid severe economic sanctions and blockade by the imperialists — the Soviet Union grew into the second largest economy in the world. Old, backward Russia entered the modern world using socialist methods of public ownership and central economic planning. It went from semi-feudalism in 1917 to a position where it launched the space age, putting the first spacecraft into orbit in 1957.

The Soviet people were among the most educated and cultured in the world. They accomplished in decades what had taken centuries to achieve in capitalist Europe.

Soviet art and culture often depicted workers, rarely seen in the West. Here, The worker and kolkhoz (collective farm) woman

For the most underdeveloped Soviet Republics in Central Asia and the Caucuses, the rate of economic and social development was even greater than that of Russia, although they still lagged behind. The Soviet Union's policies of prioritizing economic and social development in those regions were in effect the largest affirmative-action program in history.

In 1940, Hitler tried to re-impose capitalism in the Soviet Union by military force. Twenty-seven million Soviets died repelling and defeating fascism and liberating eastern and central Europe from the yoke of Nazi occupation. The Soviets never had a moment of reprieve following that awful carnage that devoured not only lives but the Soviet economic achievements of an entire post-revolutionary generation. The Cold War with the United States — which began even before World War II had ended — required a massive diversion of funds from the civilian economy to the Soviet military. Despite these setbacks and non-stop drain on resources, the Soviet economy grew quickly using socialist methods.

BEHIND GORBACHEV'S RETREAT

The eventual overthrow of the Soviet Union was not caused by economic catastrophe. The growth rate in the economy had indeed slowed by the late 1970s. The high-tech revolution that led to an across-the-board restructuring of the industrial societies in Western Europe and the United States did in fact highlight a structural problem unique to the Soviet economic system.

The widespread transfer of the newest technologies in computers and electronics into industrial production in the western capitalist powers allowed for a major contraction of the work force. Millions of industrial workers in capitalist societies lost their jobs.

In the Soviet Union, a job was a right and the government was not legally entitled to deprive workers of employment. A careful process of job training and relocation for all workers whose jobs had become redundant slowed the pace of the introduction of the new technologies. Neither Margaret Thatcher and Ronald Reagan, nor the captains of industry, experienced these inhibitions.

This structural issue came on top of the enduring problem caused by the anti-communist economic blockade that prevented any transfer to the Soviet Union of technology that was revolutionizing the means of production in the advanced capitalist societies.

Gorbachev's economic reforms known as "perestroika" were intended to use market competition as a way to end or radically diminish the Soviet government's obligations to the working class. Market forces, rather than the enshrined legal rights of the working class, would determine employment patterns.

This section of the Soviet bureaucracy represented by Gorbachev identified socialist property relations and the Soviet Union's isolation from the locomotive of the world economy as the central obstacles impeding the country from sharing in the fruits of the revolution in technology that was sweeping the world in the last quarter of the 20th century.

Gorbachev and the Soviet reformers were convinced that only by ending the Cold War and liquidating centralized economic planning would U.S. imperialism accept the Soviet Union's entry into the rapidly accelerating model of a global economy.

Partisans of the working class and those who yearn for genuine equality will remember the Soviet Union not as the end of communism but as its first grand, real-life experiment.

Instead, the reforms set forces into motion inside and outside of the Soviet Communist Party who were completely bourgeois and pro-imperialist in their orientation. The pre-existing Soviet political system had driven them underground or into the Communist Party itself.

This relatively narrow stratum, as it struggled to delegitimize and end Soviet power, did not promise the workers that they were about to loot their factories and society's wealth. They carried out the destruction of the existing government instead with a promise of ending corruption and bureaucratic abuse and bringing an end to the Cold War, which in turn would allow the people to enjoy the fruits of the world economy.

The 1917 Russian Revolution transformed private capitalist property into public property. That raised the possibility for the transition to socialism — but it hardly settled the question. It is evident by the overthrow of the socialist government that classes and class struggle do not disappear but take new forms during the post-capitalist period.

Pro-capitalist propaganda paints the high point of the 20th century as the "end of communism." Partisans of the working class and those who yearn for genuine equality will remember the Soviet Union not as the end of communism but as its first grand, real-life experiment. Its strengths and weaknesses will be assessed and incorporated by all future generations as invaluable lessons in the struggle to replace capitalist brutality, unemployment and poverty with a rational system that organizes and distributes the bounty of the world economy to meet the needs of human beings. □

Lenin, World War I and the social roots of opportunism

BY BRIAN BECKER

L **ENINISM** became fully recognized as an extension of Marxism after the success of the Russian Revolution in 1917. Throughout the world, the mass socialist parties and working class anarchist trends went through major political convulsions. New revolutionary parties, seeking to base themselves on the political and organizational lessons learned from the Bolshevik victory, were created in country after country as the left-wing socialists and anarchists split from established socialist parties and organizations to form communist parties.

But the arrival of Leninism or Bolshevism as a distinctive international extension of Marxism, in direct opposition to the accepted Marxism of the Second International, actually took shape not at the time of revolutionary victory in 1917. Rather, it happened in a period of deepest reaction: at the very start of World War I. In 1914, V.I. Lenin broke openly with "official" socialism and Marxism, declaring that the leaders of the mass socialist parties who supported their own governments at the outbreak of the war were traitors to the working class and agents of the bourgeoisie inside the working-class movement.

Although the Bolsheviks led by Lenin took shape in 1903 as an independent faction inside the Russian Social Democratic Labor Party, affiliated with the Second International, it was only in 1914 that Lenin definitively and openly broke with the International and its flagship German Social Democratic Party, then led by Karl Kautsky. The SPD had millions of members. It had a long-established left wing led by Rosa Luxemburg and Karl Liebknecht. But Kautsky was considered the principal spokesperson and theoretician of the Second International. Lenin, in spite of the Bolshevik's affinity with the German left wing, recognized Kautsky's leadership until 1914. Organized as a party of the "whole class," rather than as a disciplined revolutionary vanguard united around a political program and a political line, the German SPD and the other mass parties of the Second International had a political left wing, a right wing and a center.

Most prominent socialist leaders of the time had solemnly pledged to oppose imperialist war in powerfully written resolutions and manifestos. Most notable were the declarations of socialist conferences held in Stuttgart, Germany in 1907, and Basel, Switzerland in 1912.

When the socialist parties voted to support the war efforts of their respective governments in August 1914, it could have been explained as merely an opportunist reflex to the extreme pressure evident at the start of every imperialist war. After all, principled opposition to the war meant going directly from comfortable seats in Parliament to prison, the firing squad, or being drafted and imprisoned. Karl Liebknecht, the only member of the German SPD who voted against war credits in the Parliament, was arrested for high treason. It meant that the offices, newspapers and other publications of the party would be declared illegal and shut down. The Bolsheviks in Russia faced capital punishment trials and life-long exile in Siberia as punishment for their stand against the war in 1914, while the other ostensibly left organizations were allowed to function.

The anticipation of certain repression was only one form of pressure that the socialist leaders faced when they had to make the fateful decision in August 1914 whether to oppose the war they had promised to oppose. The other pressure — perhaps more feared than actual repression — was the fear of political isolation and contraction of support from the workers who were the base of the socialist parties.

At the start of World War I, as at the start of every imperialist war and adventure, the masses of people were whipped into a nationalist frenzy by the capitalist media. The "enemy" country was thoroughly demonized. It was one thing to be called a traitor by the bankers and bosses. It was another thing to endure the antipathy and rejection of the working people themselves.

Under these exceptional circumstances, it could be argued that it was understandable that only a handful of socialist parties stood up to the test. The Bolshevik delegates in the Duma (the czarist semi-parliament), adhering to the directions of the party center, voted against the bill authorizing the funds for war. They were sentenced to life in prison in Siberia. The leaders of the Serbian Socialist party,

Liebknecht in Germany, Monatte in France and Eugene Debs in the United States also followed this difficult path.

ROOTS OF THE BETRAYAL

Lenin, for the first time, developed an analysis proving that the opportunist betrayal by the majority of the socialist leaders in the advanced capitalist countries was neither accidental nor simply an expression of weakness in the face of pressure. Lenin not only denounced the Second International parties' capitulation at the outbreak of World War I. He also advanced for the first time a systematic materialist analysis of their retreat into national chauvinism, political opportunism and patriotism.

This analysis has a poignant relevance for the struggles going on today inside the global anti-war movement.

As a handful of capitalist nations had evolved into global imperial empires, enriching themselves at the expense of the colonized and enslaved peoples of the world, the "receipt of high monopoly profits by the capitalists ... makes it economically possible for them to bribe certain sections of the workers, and for a time a fairly considerable minority of them, and win them to the side of the bourgeoisie of a given industry or given nation against all others."[1]

The analysis of the rise of a "labor aristocracy" was first made by Friedrich Engels in the context of the political struggles inside the British working class during the second half of the nineteenth

This map illustrates the British empire in 1921, with colonies in darker gray.

century. But it was limited to the British experience and the effect of the far-flung British Empire and all of its colonial possessions on class consciousness inside Britain. Engels predicted that the labor aristocracy in Britain, and its attendant conservative influence over the bulk of the British working class, would exist only as a temporary phenomenon. It would vanish, Engels believed, as the British monopoly over industry, trade and colonies gave way to new competition.

Lenin argued that the embrace of national chauvinism and patriotic capitulation throughout the parties of the Second International proved that the rise of a politically influential labor aristocracy, no matter how small it was numerically inside the working class, was now a permanent feature in the last stage of developed capitalism — what Lenin described as monopoly capitalism or imperialism.

"The important thing is...that in the epoch of imperialism, owing to objective causes, the proletariat has been split into two international camps, one of which has been corrupted by the crumbs that fall from the table of the bourgeoisie of the dominant nations — obtained, among other things, from the double or triple exploitation of small nations," Lenin wrote.[2]

This is what laid the basis for the transformation of the leaders of the mass socialist parties to become agents of imperialism inside the ranks of the working-class movement at the outbreak of war. They were "socialists in words, imperialists in deed,"[3] Lenin and the Bolsheviks asserted from their jail cells and places of exile.

The existence of opportunism as a trend inside the socialist movement was evident before 1914. At the International Socialist Congress in 1907, a majority of delegates in a commission devoted to the colonial question adopted a draft resolution that stated, "The Congress does not in principle and for all time reject all colonial policy, which, under a socialist regime, may have a civilizing effect."[4] This wrong-headed draft resolution was eventually defeated at the Congress. Instead, the majority passed a strong resolution condemning colonialism and its inherent promotion of conquests, plunder and violence.

But Lenin, who was present at the Stuttgart conference, noted that the episode was reflective of a deeper problem. He wrote:

> Only the proletarian class, which maintains the whole of society, can bring about the social revolution.

However, as a result of the extensive colonial policy, the European proletarian partly finds himself in a position when it is not his labor, but the labor of the practically enslaved natives in the colonies, that maintains the whole of society. The British bourgeoisie, for example, derives more profit from the many millions of the population of India and other colonies than from the British workers. In certain countries this provides the material and economic basis for infecting the proletariat with colonial chauvinism. Of course, this may be only a temporary phenomenon, but the evil must nonetheless be clearly realized and its causes understood in order to be able to rally the proletariat of all countries for the struggle against such opportunism.[5]

Eight years after the Stuttgart Congress and at the beginning of World War I, Lenin concluded that the struggle against opportunism and social chauvinism was a permanent and central strategic task. He noted that a favored quote by Marx now needed amending:

The Roman proletarian lived at the expense of society. Modern society lives at the expense of the modern proletarian. ... Imperialism somewhat changes the situation. A privileged upper stratum of the proletariat in the imperialist countries lives partly at the expense of hundreds of millions in the colonized world.[6]

WHO WILL LEAD THE ANTI-WAR STRUGGLE?

The struggle against opportunism and social chauvinism is in the end a battle for leadership. On the one side are the "social" imperialists or "liberal" imperialists who retain a loyalty to the system and the political status quo. They base themselves on privileged elements of society, adhering to the capitalist system and the advantages they obtain from their position in society.

Today the broad mass of the U.S. working class is getting poorer. This section of society doesn't get a dime out of the imperialist enslavement of other countries. Wages and benefits are going down. The prison population continues to climb, with more than two million behind bars. Prison labor is becoming a bigger and bigger ingredient in the capitalist economy.

In the final analysis, the political fight against opportunism and social chauvinism is a fundamental feature of the class struggle in the epoch of imperialism. The broad working class and the revolutionary socialist organizations that seek to provide leadership in the class struggle must wage a ceaseless fight against any prejudice peddled by the capitalists and their apologists in the "loyal opposition."

The channeling of dissent into harmless safe channels is useful to the political establishment. The refusal on the part of the social imperialists in the anti-war movement to expose the imperialists as the real enemy helps keep the working class infected with the chauvinism, patriotism and racism emanating from big business propaganda.

Working-class internationalism is the only effective antidote. That was the lesson of the ultimate success of the Russian Revolution led by Lenin. It is also the key to victory in the struggle against war, racism and anti-labor attacks today. □

Lenin and the right of nations to self-determination

BY GLORIA LA RIVA

THE formation of the Union of Soviet Socialist Republics in 1922 brought together more than 120 distinct peoples, each with their own language and culture, who had been oppressed by the czar under the Russian Empire. This great achievement grew out of the Russian Revolution of 1917. It would not have been possible without a profound struggle to overcome national oppression and a correct position on what was then referred to as "the national question."

It was Karl Marx who first expressed the position of the communist movement on the national question. In 1848, when the Communist Manifesto was written, bourgeois-democratic revolutions had exploded throughout Europe against autocratic, reactionary monarchies and empires like the Austro-Hungarian, Prussian and Russian empires. These revolutions were led by the rising bourgeoisie against feudalism.

Marx and his co-thinker, Frederick Engels, stood for fighting all forms of oppression. Their goal was to organize the workers to overthrow capitalism worldwide and establish socialism. Marx and Engels saw the national bourgeois-democratic struggles as progressive, because they were the inevitable and necessary step in the revolutionary development of capitalism over feudalism. Unification into nation-states laid the basis for the development of capitalism and the further development of the growing working class.

MARX AND IRELAND

Marx's analysis of the Irish question was one of his most important contributions on the issue of self-determination for oppressed nations. Marx at first did not think the Irish nation could achieve independence alone, or that it should. He thought the Irish

The aftermath of the Burning of Cork by the British
during the Irish War of Independence, December, 1920

nation and workers would be liberated when English workers overthrew the English bourgeoisie.

The way he saw it, the English workers lived in an advanced
capitalist country and were in a more advantageous position to overthrow capitalism in the colonizing country of Britain. That was how
he envisioned the emancipation of the Irish at first.

But by the late 1860s, Marx recognized the virulent racism
and chauvinism among the English workers themselves against Irish
people. He came to support self-determination and independence for
the Irish nation as the best means for the Irish workers to fight capitalism. He urged the English workers to stand up for Irish independence.

Furthermore, Marx argued that an English workers' party, representing workers from an oppressor nation, had the duty to support
an oppressed nation's self-determination and independence. This attitude became a very key part of Lenin's view on the national question
as it relates to oppressed nations.

This view recognized that even when the English workers did
not benefit materially from their bourgeoisie's oppression of Ireland,
they still had become infected with their ruling class' chauvinism and
racism. So it was the English workers' party's duty to fight colonialism.

English workers could never attain liberation as long as the Irish continued to be oppressed. It was similar to his view about the United States, when Marx said during the time of slavery, "Labor in white skin will never be free as long as labor in [B]lack skin is branded."[1]

Lenin was later to write, "The policy of Marx and Engels on the Irish question serves as a splendid example of the attitude the proletariat of the oppressor nations should adopt towards national movements, an example which has lost none of its immense practical importance."[2]

Lenin, continuing the Marxist approach, had to struggle over and over with other socialists who were opposed in principle to the right of national self-determination.

This was mainly because some of these social-democratic parties were petty-bourgeois and greatly influenced by the fact that they lived in empires like the Austro-Hungarian or Russian empires at that time. They did not see independence as viable for other smaller nations. Lenin more than once referred to these socialists as "Great Nation chauvinists," that is, that they identified with the dominant nation's oppression over other nations.

THE RUSSIAN EMPIRE: 'PRISON HOUSE OF NATIONS'

Lenin's profound understanding of the national question was aided by the fact that he was from Russia, the most multinational state of the time. czarist Russia was not a nation; it was a state composed of 200 nationalities and languages. It was known as Russia because of the dominance of the "Great Russian" nation. The term "Great Russian" was used to distinguish the dominant nationality from the White Russians of Belarus or the Ukrainians.

These three Slavic nations were in fact very closely related. A person from the Great Russian nationality could understand the language of a White Russian or a Ukrainian. Great Russians made up about 45 percent of the whole population. The three main Slavic nations were 110 million out of the 140 million at the turn of the century. All the other nationalities made up about 30 million, compared to 60 million Great Russians.

The ethnic diversity of the empire, and later the Soviet Union, was truly amazing. But the experience of the minority nationalities before the revolution was common: institutionalized oppression.

Their languages were often banned. Some peoples had no written language. Most people in the oppressed nations could not read or write.

Czarist Russia was known as the "prison house of nations" because of the very brutal and autocratic rule by the czarist nobility over the many subjected peoples. Russian workers and peasants were oppressed as workers and peasants. But the other nationalities — Georgians, Azerbaijanis or Turkic peoples and the others — suffered extra oppression.

The state religion was Orthodox Christianity. Jews were denied all rights. Muslims were considered religious enemies. Even when the czar was forced to concede a Parliament — the Duma — after the 1905 Revolution, Muslims were not allowed to vote.

Corliss Lamont, in his book "The Peoples of the Soviet Union," quoted a Muslim cotton grower describing the relations before the 1917 Revolution in what later became Turkmenistan: "The past was a stairway of years carpeted with pain. The Uzbeks feared to go along the street of the Arabs; the Tajiks carried sticks when they walked through the Uzbek quarter." Yet they were all Muslim.

Jews also suffered tremendous oppression. Under the czar, there were over 100 laws that denied Jews basic rights. They could not own land or work in agriculture, they could not be in government, work in the post office or on the railroads. They were victims of pogroms — large-scale massacres unleashed by the czar.

The biggest problem that many of the nations faced was extreme underdevelopment and feudal conditions. Among some of the Central Asian nationalities, women were treated as property who could be killed if they dared to read or write.

IS WORKING-CLASS UNITY POSSIBLE?

For Lenin, as leader of the Bolsheviks, the question was how to develop a party and lead a revolution in such a multinational state, with all the divisions among the nationalities and peoples, with all the oppression experienced at the hands of the Great Russian nation, with all the mistrust and understandable resentment toward the Great Russians of all classes. How could the Bolsheviks build the unity of all workers and oppressed peoples that was necessary in order to overthrow the czar and build socialism?

The formal view of many Marxists of that time was, "All workers are workers, all poor peasants are poor peasants, we should all unite!"

But the real situation required more than such formal and mechanical declarations. Simply saying "unite," meant ignoring the national oppression and virulent racism faced by the oppressed nations.

> Simply saying 'unite," meant ignoring the national oppression and virulent racism faced by the oppressed nations.

The Great Russian nation denied language rights and culture, and imposed greater taxes against others. This chauvinism by the nobility infected the Russian workers and peasants. In turn, all the oppressed peoples were deeply resentful of this racism and repression.

How, Lenin asked, could there be real unity under these circumstances between the workers of the oppressor nationality and the workers of the other nationalities?

THE RIGHT OF SELF-DETERMINATION

For Lenin, the key was for the Great Russian working class and the revolutionary party to make clear their unequivocal opposition to every manifestation of Great Russian oppression, privilege and racism. The party had to be the leader in fighting for equality of language rights, equality of education and of cultural rights. He was confident that the unity would come about when the oppressed peoples, especially the workers and peasants, were confident that the Bolsheviks were committed to self-determination and equality.

Lenin said that the party must show that it fights to eliminate all the deeply embedded biases and privileges connected with being Great Russians. In notes dictated in December 1922, he observed that:

"[W]e nationals of a big nation, have nearly always been guilty, in historic practice, of an infinite number of cases of violence; furthermore, we commit violence and insult an infinite number of times without noticing it. ...

"That is why internationalism on the part of oppressors or 'great' nations, as they are called (though they are great only in their violence, only great as bullies), must consist not only in the observance of the formal equality of nations but even in an inequality of the oppressor nation, the great nation, that must make up for the inequality which it obtains in actual practice."[3]

To make it completely clear that the revolutionary workers' party was committed to ending national oppression, it must also support the right of the oppressed nation to separate to form its own state. That did not mean that socialists advocate for a separate state in every instance; in some cases, socialists might argue the inadvisability of an independent state or the benefits of union. But they must be uncompromising in their rejection of bourgeois "unity" as a cover for continued national oppression and subjugation by "great" nations.

Unity, if there was to be unity, must be on a completely voluntary basis, stated Lenin. Its most important prerequisite is the commitment of party members from the oppressor nationality to fight energetically against national oppression and racism.

At the same time, he called for party members from the oppressed nationalities to fight for working-class internationalism. He warned against any concessions to bourgeois nationalism, which "joins the proletarians and bourgeoisie of one nation and keeps the proletarians of different nations apart."[4]

"Workers who place political unity with 'their own' bourgeoisie above complete unity with the proletariat of all nations are acting against their own interests, against the interests of socialism and against the interests of democracy."[5]

WORLD WAR I AND THE STRUGGLE AGAINST IMPERIALISM

With the outbreak of World War I in 1914, clarity on the socialist perspective toward oppressed nationalities became more important than ever.

All of the major imperialist empires and powers joined in the war. All evoked national chauvinism to motivate their respective working classes to fight other workers so that the imperialists could re-divide the world. Lenin showed that the imperialists were not fighting to defend self-determination but to annex other countries, and that it was more important than ever to defend smaller countries' right to independence.

Even as Lenin insisted on self-determination for all nations, he also saw that with the first imperialist world war, the contradictions of capitalism had brought the socialist revolution closer. He had to grapple with a further developing reality in the world: That some areas were far more advanced in the capitalist phase than others.

By 1914, the continents of Africa, Asia and Latin America had been carved up and divided among the imperialist powers. Lenin wrote his monumental works on the implications of this period and the relationship between the struggle inside the imperialist countries and the anti-colonial struggles.

In April 1916, Lenin wrote "The Socialist Revolution and the Rights of Nations to Self-determination." He said that society had reached a level of objective development where socialism was now possible and within reach. The victorious socialist countries' first task would be to complete the extension of bourgeois democratic rights for the population, and would have to recognize the right of oppressed nations to self-determination.

Lenin described three types of countries:

> First, the advanced capitalist countries of Western Europe and the United States. The tasks of the proletariat of these ruling nations are the same as those of the proletariat in England in the nineteenth century in relation to Ireland.

> Secondly, Eastern Europe: Austria, the Balkans and particularly Russia. Here it was the 20th century that particularly developed the bourgeois-democratic national movements and intensified the national struggle. The most difficult and most important task in this is to unite the class struggle of the workers of the oppressor nations with that of the workers of the oppressed nations.

> Thirdly, the semi-colonial countries, such as China, Persia and Turkey, and all the colonies which have a combined population of 1,000 million people. Socialists must not only demand the unconditional and immediate liberation of the colonies without compensation ... they must also render determined support to the more revolutionary elements in the bourgeois-democratic movements

for national liberation in these countries and assist their uprising — or revolutionary war, in the event of one — against the imperialist powers that oppressed them.

In Lenin's 1916 pamphlet, "Imperialism: The Highest Stage of Capitalism," he wrote that the struggle of the semi-colonial and colonial countries was no longer in most cases against feudalism, but against imperialism.

A 1947 Soviet one-ruble bill, with the denomination marked in 15 languages

On Nov. 7, 1917, the Bolsheviks came to power, overthrowing the capitalist Kerensky government in the greatest social upheaval ever in history. That monumental event was the first step in ending national oppression and freeing all workers and peasants from class rule. The Bolsheviks did not think this was the end of the process.

With the victory of the revolution, the material basis of the oppression of nationalities was over. Not a week passed before the Bolsheviks laid out a whole new series of revolutionary decrees and institutions designed to bring about equality among nations and end centuries of oppression.

First, the People's Commissariat of Nationalities — known as Narkomnats — was established to deal with issues and matters concerning any particular nationality, with a member of each nationality to direct the issue. For the distinct regions of the vast territory of the former Russian empire, the Bolsheviks' approach took into account the specific histories and cultures of the peoples.

For example, much of the eastern lands of northern Caucasus and Central Asia were comprised of Turkmens, Uzbeks, Kazakhs, Kirgiz and Chechens, who were predominantly Muslim. On December 7, 1917, the Bolsheviks issued a stirring appeal, "To All Muslim Toilers of Russia and East:"

Muslims of Russia, Tatars of the Volga and the Crimea, Kirghiz, and Sarts of Siberia and Turkestan, Turks and Tatars of Transcaucasia, Chechens and Mountaineers of the Caucasus — all you whose mosques and oratories have been destroyed, whose beliefs and customs have been trampled underfoot by the czars and the oppressors of Russia: Your beliefs and usages, your national and cultural institutions are henceforth free and inviolable. Build your national life in complete freedom. You have the right to do so. Know that your rights, like those of all the peoples of Russia, are under the powerful safeguard of the revolution and of its organs, the Soviets of workers, soldiers and peasants. Defend this revolution and its plenipotentiary government!

The statement, unprecedented in its unconditional support, was the attitude imparted by Lenin of the need for workers in the Great Russian state, historically the oppressor nation, to break with all the czar had done to the Eastern peoples. The workers' and peasants' government was determined to show that trust and workers' solidarity could overcome all obstacles.

The next three difficult years, characterized by civil war and imperialist invasion, provide many rich lessons in how the Bolshevik policy on national oppression was put into practice. After these conflicts subsided, the new Soviet state was then able to fully carry out the vital task of socialist construction and equality of the nationalities. □

Revolutionary woman and educator

Nadezhda Krupskaya

BY CANDICE YANEZ

NADEZHDA Krupskaya was a Russian Bolshevik revolutionary. A feminist who contributed to the women's question, Krupskaya was also involved in establishing International Women's Day. Her contributions to educational policy and theory were so immense that the Soviet Union, from 1970-1992, sponsored UNESCO Nadezhda K. Krupskaya literacy prize in her honor.

Krupskaya was born in St. Petersburg on February 26, 1869. Impoverished for most of her early life, she was aware of the injustices in the world. Krupskaya's childhood was shaped by the revolutionary air of late-19th century Russia. In the book, "Bride of the Revolution: Krupskaya and Lenin," biographer Robert H. McNeal declares that Krupskaya's early life and experiences naturally shaped her into a vital revolutionary, "She was virtually born to this vocation, the only child of a radical man and an emancipated woman. If Krupskaya's life entitles her to be called the bride of the revolution, her birth entitles her to be called a daughter of the revolution."

Krupskaya's parents had gentry class origins yet were not wealthy. Both were progressives, influencing Krupskaya's early interest in revolutionary politics. Education was one of her earliest passions. In her youth, she was particularly interested in Leo Tolstoy's theory of democratic education, and her concern with education pushed her to enter the teaching profession. Before becoming involved in revolutionary politics, she worked as a governess for noble families. In 1894, the combination of her studious nature and revolutionary spirit led to her involvement in an underground study group on Marxist theories. It is here that she met Vladimir Lenin. Shortly after meeting, Krupskaya and Lenin started organizing factory workers.

Krupskaya and Lenin at a retreat, 1922. The gun barrel indicated a continuing need to protect the revolution.

PHOTO: MARIA ULYANOVA

Following Lenin's arrest in 1895, Krupskaya was arrested in 1896 for her organizing work. Both were exiled to Siberia, where they married. Later, in 1903, the couple moved to Geneva, where Krupskaya worked on the editorial board of Iskra, the newspaper of the Russian Social Democratic Labour Party. In 1905, Krupskaya worked as secretary of the Central Committee of the party, and also as editorial secretary for the party's journals. Throughout her lifetime, Krupskaya worked on thousands of pamphlets, articles and books.

KRUPSKAYA'S CONTRIBUTIONS TO THE WOMAN'S QUESTION AND EDUCATIONAL THEORY

Krupskaya wrote extensively on the woman's question. "The Woman Worker," written while she was still in exile and published in 1901, is considered a landmark in revolutionary literature on women's liberation. The article describes the abject poverty and suffering of peasant and working women. Although it had to be smuggled into Russia, the article became popular for its accessible Marxist analysis. It was used to organize factory workers and influenced Lenin and the party to focus more closely on women's liberation. In 1910, Krupskaya, Inessa Armand and Clara Zetkin founded International Women's Day. International Women's Day was originally celebrated on the last Sunday in February and was first observed in 1913. Krupskaya insisted that the struggle for women's liberation was essential for a successful revolution. International Women's Day was not only intended to be a celebration of women, but a way to motivate the working class into action. She wrote of this in her article for the first issue of the women's journal, Rabotnitsa:

> That which unites working women with working men is stronger than that which divides them. They are united by their common lack of rights, their common needs, their common condition, which is struggle and their common goal. ... Solidarity between working men and working women, common activity, a common goal, a common path to this goal — such is the solution of the 'woman' question among workers.

After the 1917 Revolution, Krupskaya focused on her role as deputy to the People's Commissar of Education. She is lauded for her contributions to Marxist educational theory, articulated in writings such as "Concerning the Question of Socialist Schools" published in 1918. In this essay, Krupskaya advocates socialism as the only way to transform the school system into one accessible to all and to serve the working class:

> In serving the interests of the masses the government of workers and peasants must break the schools' class character and make schools at all levels accessible to all sections of the population. It must do this not in words but in deeds. Until the objectives of schools are changed, education will remain a class privilege of the bourgeoisie.

Krupskaya practiced Marxist educational theory and translated it into action and policy. Eradicating illiteracy became one of her main concerns, since "economically and culturally we can develop no further without dispelling the darkness of illiteracy."[1] Krupskaya tackled this issue by initiating adult education programs, which provided 30,000 classes for peasants and factory workers across the Soviet Union. Her work within education helped the Soviet Union significantly reduce illiteracy.

Nadezhda Krupskaya passed away on February 27, 1939. She is an example of disciplined devotion to the revolution, and her legacy is particularly relevant today with a new burgeoning women's movement. She is a reminder of the broader context of the women's struggle, the fact that women's liberation is inseparable from the entire working-class movement. Krupskaya and the other revolutionaries who established International Women's Day did so with the intention of uniting these two struggles. Given the current push to privatize education in the United States, it is important to remember Krupskaya's fight to create a public educational system accessible to all, from primary school to higher education. Her tireless work, from education to women's rights, makes her a hero to our class. She provides a model of dedication that we should seek to emulate. □

Celebrating International Women's Day

BY ALEXANDRA KOLLONTAI

Alexandra Kollontai (1872-1952) was a Russian communist organizer. She was exiled for conducting underground political work in 1908, but returned to Russia after the February 1917 revolution.

To commemorate International Women's Day is this excerpt from Kollontai's 1920 article, "International Women's Day," written just two years after the October 1917 socialist revolution in Russia. The entire article can be found at www.marxists.org.

WOMEN'S Day, or Working Women's Day, is a day of international solidarity, and a day for reviewing the strength and organization of proletarian women.

But this is not a special day for women alone. The 8th of March is a historic and memorable day for the workers and peasants, for all the Russian workers and for the workers of the whole world. In 1917, on this day, the great February revolution broke out. It was the working women of Petersburg who began this revolution; it was they who first decided to raise the banner of opposition to the czar and his associates. And so, working women's day is a double celebration for us.

PURPOSE OF WOMEN'S DAY

[Women's Day] turned out above all to be an excellent method of agitation among the less political of our proletarian sisters. They could not help but turn their attention to the meetings, demonstrations, posters, pamphlets and newspapers that were devoted to Women's Day. Even the politically backward working woman thought to herself: "This is our day, the festival for working women," and she hurried to the meetings and demonstrations. After each Working Women's Day, more

Alexandra Kollontai, seated at left.

women joined the socialist parties and the trade unions grew. Organizations improved and political consciousness developed.

These are the results of working women's day of militancy. The day of working women's militancy helps increase the consciousness and organization of proletarian women. And this means that its contribution is essential to the success of those fighting for a better future for the working class.

"Working Women's Day" was first organized ten years ago in the campaign for the political equality of women and the struggle for socialism. This aim has been achieved by the working-class women in Russia. In the Soviet Republic the working women and peasants do not need to fight for the franchise and for civil rights.

RIGHTS ALONE ARE NOT ENOUGH

But rights alone are not enough. We have to learn to make use of them. The right to vote is a weapon which we have to learn to master for our own benefit, and for the good of the workers' republic. In the two years of Soviet power, life itself has not been absolutely changed. We are only in the process of struggling for communism and we are surrounded by the world we have inherited from the dark and repressive past. Working women and peasant women can only rid themselves of this situation and achieve equality in life itself, and not just in law, if they put all their energies into making Russia a truly communist society.

After the experience of the Russian October Revolution, it is clear to every working woman in France, in England and in other countries that only the dictatorship of the working class, only the power of the soviets can guarantee complete and absolute equality, the ultimate victory of communism will tear down the century-old chains of repression and lack of rights.

Only the overthrow of capitalism and the establishment of Soviet power will save them from the world of suffering, humiliations and inequality that makes the life of the working woman in the capitalist countries so hard. The Working Woman's Day turns from a day of struggle for the franchise into an international day of struggle for the full and absolute liberation of women, which means a struggle for the victory of the Soviets and for communism! ☐

Black Bolsheviks and white lies

BY PETA LINDSAY

A **LOT** of nonsense has been written about the role of Putin's Russia in subverting "our democracy." As though our democracy had been functioning perfectly or even reasonably well until these shadowy Russian forces purchased a few Facebook ads that sent us all into the streets. It is a laughable concept. I am sorry, did Putin acquit George Zimmerman or Jason Stockley? Did Putin shoot 12-year-old Tamir Rice? Russia did not carry out the drug war against African Americans or implement policies of mass incarceration, or pass voter ID laws in the United States, all of which have contributed to disenfranchising millions of African Americans over the years. The United States has a lot to answer for in regard to systematically denying the democratic rights of African Americans. This is not the first time they have tried to deflect criticism for that by blaming Russia. As a student of history I have mostly just rolled my eyes this time around while the Democrats attempt to make red-scare tactics that are very old, new again. But a recent entry in this canon of "Black activists are pawns of Moscow" writing is so insulting and patently false, that, as we approach the hundredth anniversary of the Russian Revolution, it seems very important to reply.

On Sept. 28, 2017, an author named Terrell Jermaine Starr wrote a piece for The Root entitled, "Russia's Recent Facebook Ads Prove the Kremlin Never Loved Black People."

I have enjoyed entries from The Root before, particularly in chronicling racist attacks against African Americans that are underreported in the mainstream media. But their willingness to toe the Democratic Party line, uncritically in most circumstances, has been noted.

Starr's piece is supposedly historical in scope but is premised upon a huge, glaring, historical fallacy: conflating the Russian Fed-

Peta Lindsay, 2012 presidential candidate of the Party for Socialism and Liberation

eration with the Soviet Union. In one sentence, Starr describes the two as essentially the same (showing you the level of material historical analysis in which he is interested in engaging) and then for the rest of the article proceeds to whitewash the history of Black communism, using the favorite arguments deployed by racists — that Blacks who supported socialism did so because they were duped, and that the Soviet Union was only interested in Black liberation insofar as it meant spiting their enemies in the White House.

These assertions deny the agency of African Americans, many of whom were amongst the most prominent Black intellectuals of their time, who looked to the Soviet system as an alternative to American racism and exploitation. This interpretation also denies the real solidarity and support that the Soviet Union expressed in their assistance to liberation movements of many Black, brown and oppressed people all over the world. Since anti-communist propaganda is easily promulgated without evidence in this country, allow me to present some of the evidence that exposes these racist lies for what they are.

The Union of Soviet Socialist Republics was birthed via a revolution in 1917 and overthrown via counter-revolution in 1991. While Russians were in the majority of the population, the USSR itself was actually an extremely diverse and vibrant society for all of its existence. The Soviet Union spanned 14 time zones and comprised many independent nationalities and ethnic groups, such as Tajiks, Kazakhs, Lithuanians, Tartars — all of whom spoke different languages, practiced different religions — and suffered terrible racist oppression under the czar. The triumph of the socialist October Revolution and the very existence of this unique political formation was the result of a revolution carried out by united oppressed peoples, who rose up as one and took control of society away from their czarist and capitalist exploiters. The Bolsheviks always took the task of uniting oppressed people and elevating their struggle very seriously. This was a key to their success and a guiding principle in their work. It was Lenin who pioneered

In what was known as 'Red Summer, a white mob drags a Black family from their car in Detroit, 1919.

communist opposition to imperialism and he who changed the Marxist formulation, "Workers of the world unite" to "Workers and oppressed people of the world unite" as an expression of the priority they placed on the struggle of colonized people against imperialism.

Around the world, the triumph of the Bolsheviks was greeted by the imperialists with great dismay and by oppressed/colonized peoples with great enthusiasm, inspiration and hope. In America, 1919 was an infamous year, known for its "Red Summer" of intense lynchings, race riots and gruesome violence against African Americans at the hands of white mobs. The Black American political movement had entered a new era of militancy, as veterans returning from WWI were less inclined to submit to Jim Crow and more inclined to fight for their dignity, wages and rights. In the 1920s and 30s, a new wave of radical Black intellectuals all but took over the Black political scene, many from the Caribbean and mostly based in Harlem. These men and women were considered some of the premier thinkers and writers of their time and the majority of these radical African American leaders

— regardless of political orientation — held the Russian Revolution in very high esteem.

According to historian Winston James, in his work "Holding Aloft the Banner of Ethiopia," the appeal of the Russian Revolution to Black people in America at the time lay not in their having been "recruited" by Russia as The Root article asserts, but in their own independent evaluation of the Bolshevik government and where it stood with regard to equality for oppressed and colonized people.

James wrote about three major factors that attracted Black people to Bolshevism in the 1920s and 30s. The first was the domestic policies promoting national minorities and oppressed groups that were put in place almost immediately after the triumph of the revolution. After the revolution the Bolshevik government undertook what can be described as the most far-reaching and thorough affirmative action plan that any government has ever attempted. The socialist government dedicated much in the way of their limited resources towards raising the standard of living for groups who had been historically oppressed by creating conditions that could facilitate greater equality for those groups.

To Black Americans, the most convincing example was the swiftness and seriousness with which the Soviets began redressing historical inequality suffered by Jewish people, including immediately outlawing discrimination against them and putting an end to the violent pogroms that had plagued them under the czar. In 1923 Claude McKay, the young Black intellectual, writer and poet wrote: "For American Negroes the indisputable and outstanding fact of the Russian Revolution is that a mere handful of Jews, much less in ratio to the number of Negroes in the American population, have attained, through the Revolution, all the political and social rights that were denied to them under the regime of the czar."[1]

The other two factors explored by James were the "uncompromising rhetoric of anti-colonialism, anti-imperialism, and the right of self-determination for oppressed nations"[2] espoused by the Bolshevik government and the creation of the Third Communist International, an international body that openly encouraged colonized (often Black or brown) people to rise up against their (mostly European) exploiters all over the world.

The U.S. government had systematically ignored the pleas of Black people to pass even one federal law against lynching, when city and state governments all over the country were colluding in lynchings, race riots and allowing whites who attacked Blacks to go free, or even reap rewards. It does not take a genius to figure out why many Black thinkers were genuinely excited that such a different kind of government, one that spoke to them and had taken action to support and defend its own national minorities, had come into the world.

BLACK AND WHITE (FILM)

Langston Hughes was a Black intellectual of this generation, the same generation that we associate with the Harlem Renaissance and the New Negro. Of all the insults buried in that heinous Root article, the disrespect to Langston Hughes, inarguably one of the greatest American writers of the 20th century, is one of the most difficult to endure. Starr paints Hughes as a dupe, someone "recruited" to champion the Soviet Union, as if the man had not traveled all over the world, studied and written extensively and was not capable of genuinely supporting a government that he believed to be on the right track. We revere Hughes' poetry that celebrates Black beauty, he is the jazz poet laureate of Black America and we love to recite his words that

Langston Hughes

affirm our deep history and continued struggle in the face of white American racism. But what about his poetry celebrating the Soviet Union? Hughes wrote a poem praising Lenin entitled "Ballads of Lenin."[3] Did they break that one out at your school's Black history month event? Probably not. But that does not change the fact that Langston Hughes was extremely sympathetic to the Soviet Union, as is abundantly evident in his autobiographical writing, "I Wonder As I Wander," in the chapter "Moscow Movie."

The Root provides perhaps the most cynical and shallow reading of this chapter possible, though I hesitate to affirm that the author of that piece has even actually read it. "Moscow Movie" tells an important story about a time in 1932 when Langston Hughes was invited to the Soviet Union by the government, to work on a major film production. This film was called "Black and White" and it was supposed to highlight the struggle of Black workers in the South and give an international showcase to the racism and oppression experienced by Black people in America. According to Langston Hughes, it was "intended to be the first great Negro-white film ever made in the world,"[4] though unfortunately it did not come to fruition.

Hughes accompanied a delegation of 22 young African Americans who were supposed to star in the film, though it was odd that most in that group were not actors or performers by trade. Starr erroneously attributes this casting to racism, saying that Hughes determined that the Soviets were so racist that they assumed that all Black people could sing and dance (and play sports?), and so did not bother to check the backgrounds of the people they hired for the film.

In fact, Hughes said nothing of the sort. He addressed the peculiar composition of the delegation early in the chapter, stating, "That most of our group were not actors seems to have been due to the fact that very few professional theater people were willing to pay their own fares to travel all the way to Russia to sign contracts they had never seen. Only a band of eager, adventurous young students, teachers, writers and would-be-actors were willing to do that, looking forward to the fun and wonder of a foreign land as much as to film-making. There were a few among them who wanted to get away from American race prejudice forever, being filled up with Jim Crow."[5]

It's important that Hughes highlighted their motives as traveling to seek a reprieve from American racism. So high was the esteem for the Soviet Union in the group, that "when the train stopped beneath this banner for passports to be checked, a few of the young [B]lack men and women left the train to touch their hands to Soviet soil, lift the new earth in their palms, and kiss it,"[6] according to Hughes.

In his accusations of racism what Starr may be referring to is where Hughes says at one point, "Europeans as well as Americans, seem to be victims of that old cliche that Negroes just naturally sing."[7] That is hardly an indictment of any particularly Russian racism and more of a complaint on how African Americans are represented on the world stage.

Lack of specific cultural knowledge about African Americans was a problem throughout the film's production and that is what Hughes believes ultimately damned the film. Hughes was given an early copy of the script and let them know that he did not think it was usable because there were so many errors with regard to what racism and working-class struggle actually looked like in the American South. Hughes said that the author of the script was well-intentioned but had never been to America. He also said that information from or by Black Americans was rarely translated into Russian in those days. Even with these critiques, it's nearly impossible to interpret Hughes as being at all bitter or resentful at the Soviets for their attempt at making this film. On the contrary, Hughes wrote with unmistakable good humor throughout the chapter and also repeatedly mentioned that they were all paid in full and well taken care of, even when it became clear the film would not be made.

The reception that the students received in Moscow is really remarkable, especially considering the historical context — none of which The Root brings up, of course. The students were "wined and dined" in Hughes' own words, they were put up in the most lavish hotels and treated to free tickets to the theater, opera, ballet and dinners and parties with dignitaries and important people almost every night. They were official guests of the state and treated with the highest honors. No Black delegation has ever been received in America with such grace. Hughes says that they were always introduced as "representatives of the great Negro people"[8] and after describing the incredible amenities at one of the elaborate resorts they were housed in, he adds "I had never stayed in such a hotel in my own country, since, as a rule, Negroes were not then permitted to do so."[9]

On their reception by ordinary Soviet citizens, Hughes writes in "I Wonder as I Wander":

> Of all the big cities in the world where I've been, the Muscovites seemed to me to be the politest of peoples to strangers. But perhaps that was because we were Negroes and, at that time, with the Scottsboro Case on world-wide trial in the papers everywhere, and especially in Russia, folks went out of their way there to show us courtesy. On a crowded bus, nine times out of ten, some Russian would

say, 'Negrochanski tovarish — Negro comrade — take my seat!' On the streets queueing up for newspapers or cigarettes, or soft drinks, often folks in line would say, 'Let the Negro comrade go forward.'

This is in 1932! Nowhere in America were Black people treated like this in 1932. Hell, many of us could not get that treatment today, if our lives depended on it (and they sometimes do). This account echoes many others by African Americans who visited or moved to the Soviet Union. In William Mandel's "Soviet but Not Russian," Muhammad Ali is quoted as saying of his 1978 visit to the Soviet Union:

I saw a hundred nationalities. No such thing as a Black man, or a white man, or 'you nigger,' or get back. People say, 'Oh well, they just showed you the best.' You mean all of those white folks rehearsed, said: 'Muhammad Ali's coming!' ... 'All hundred nationalities, pretend you get along. Muhammad Ali's coming!' ... 'They just took you where they wanted to go.'

I know that's a lie. I got in my car and told my driver where to go. Lying about the Russians.. I jogged in the mornings in strange places where they hardly ever saw a Black man. I ran past two little white Russian ladies who were walking to work. They didn't look around and ask what I was doing. I can't go jogging in some streets in America in the morning in a white neighborhood.

The Root tries to paint a picture of a USSR where the same racism that existed in Jim Crow America infected everyone there, but there simply is not enough evidence to say that was the case. They cite the experiences of one Black American man (Robert Robinson), thoroughly. What about the experiences of the estimated 400,000 African students who were educated for free in the Soviet Union from 1950 to 1990? These Black youth attended technical schools, Lumumba University and the special Lenin school for leadership; they lived and traveled all over the Soviet Union and upon graduation, they would return to their homelands with skills necessary to aid in the new inde-

Wilhelmina Scott Boyle, speaking at the celebration of International Women's Day on March 8, 1972 at the Patrice Lumumba People's Friendship University.

pendence governments. Mandel interviewed quite a few Black Soviets for his book, including other African Americans who moved to the Soviet Union and the picture they paint is very different from the one in Robinson's account. Providing no evidence, Starr also asserts that interracial relationships would naturally be a problem in the Soviet Union, saying "both Russian and white American men weren't cool with their women messing with [B]lack men." Since he introduced the term "bullshit" just before that line, I'm going to call bullshit on that.

Langston Hughes' account features many stories of the men in his group dating Soviet women and not a word about anyone batting an eye at such pairings, which in 1932, would have gotten someone lynched in the United States. Please stop projecting American racism onto the Soviet Union, when you just do not have the evidence to back that up. As W.E.B. Dubois wrote on his third visit to the USSR in 1949, "of all countries, Russia alone has made race prejudice a crime; of all great imperialisms, Russia alone owns no colonies of dark serfs or white and what is more important has no investments in colonies and is lifting no blood-soaked profits from cheap labor in Asia and Africa."[10] The material basis for widespread Jim Crow style racism just was not there.

Hughes was aware that the Western press celebrated the failure of the movie and spread many rumors that they knew to be false concerning the Soviet government maneuvering against the Black students. He writes that Western journalists, who saw them spending money and carousing in Moscow nightclubs, filed stories in the United States about how they were going unpaid and neglected.

Hughes wrote that some in his group suspected that the movie was scrapped because the Soviets were sacrificing the Black struggle to appease the American government — but Hughes himself did not believe that. He was one of the only members of the group who saw the script and he was unequivocal in stating that more than anything else, it was the script that caused the project's failure. Hughes also repeatedly mentioned the context of the international campaign in defense of the Scottsboro Boys, a Black struggle that was most certainly not being dropped by the Soviets, as all this was going on.

The Root miscasts this excerpt from the life of Langston Hughes to support their conclusion that "the Soviets' attempts to curry favor with the Black struggle" was "insincere and downright fraudulent." I would counter that this anti-communist propaganda is actually "insincere and downright fraudulent" but allow me to present further evidence on the genuine solidarity expressed by the Soviet Union. Sticking with the theme, let's keep talking about film.

FOCUS ON AFRICA IN FILM

In the book "Focus on African Film," noted film scholar Josephine Woll describes "The Russian Connection" between the Soviet Union and African film, an invaluable alliance in making post-colonial African cinema a reality. As alluded to in the previous section, the Soviet Union expended a lot of resources on aid and development for African nations, who were in the process of throwing off their own colonial oppressors and beginning their independence after World War II. These countries were severely underdeveloped, as chronicled by Walter Rodney, and the Soviet Union was a key ally in providing material support, education and technology to allow these countries to thrive without being beholden to their former colonial masters. It is worth noting that the greatest victory for Black liberation to occur in my lifetime, the fall of apartheid in South Africa, involved a great deal of material and political support from the Soviet Union, which was integral to the success of that movement.

Film was another area in which the Soviet Union provided Africans with crucial foundational support. Ousmane Sembene of Senegal, widely considered the "father of African film," was educated in the Soviet Union. This was also the case for other pioneering African filmmakers, like Souleymane Cissé of Mali and Abderrahmne Sissako of Mauritania/Mali and Sarah Maldoror, the French daughter of immigrants from Guadeloupe who made many films about African liberation. In addition to technical know-how, the Soviet Union also provided the essential film and production equipment, distribution and promotion, to bring African cinema onto the world stage.

Ousmane Sembene

Dr. Woll seems to believe that the motives of the Soviets were clearly political, but also genuine. Woll wrote: "The Bolshevik Revolution and its aftermath, radically altered how, why, and for whom films were made. Financial profit still mattered but it competed with other goals: educational, political, promotional. The new regime in post-czarist Russia, like the new leaders of post-colonial African nations, willingly allocated part of its budget to subsidizing cinema because it recognized how effective the medium could be as an instrument of propaganda; and most Soviet filmmakers in the 1920s, though they had individual and often compelling aesthetic agendas, readily supported the politics of revolution." In the United States we tend to be very cynical of the word "propaganda" but in revolutionary times, propaganda is necessary and the Africans needed aid in producing theirs. Ousmane Sembene clearly agreed; he was adamant about telling compelling political stories through his films and he fully recognized the potential for his films to "help decolonize Africa."

The Soviet Union trained and equipped these African directors, so that they could bring the beauty and the struggle of their people to the world stage. The work of these revolutionary African filmmakers can be seen as a happy ending to the saga that was begun with "Black and White." While we never got the Soviet-sponsored film about the Black struggle in the United States that they wanted to produce, we have since seen a variety of films out of different African countries that highlight their struggle in similar, but undoubtedly much more accurate, ways.

CONCLUSION

I realize that this was a lot to write in response to a small article that was probably not even this carefully considered by the author himself. But the legacy of the Soviet Union with regard to the Black struggle is unique and inspiring and should be celebrated, not horrifically distorted and denied. In "Paul Robeson Speaks," the great Black American actor says:

> Mankind has never witnessed the equal of the Constitution of the U.S.S.R. ... Firstly, because of the significance it has for my people generally. Everywhere else, outside of the Soviet world, [B]lack men are an oppressed and inhumanely exploited people. Here, they come within the provisions of Article 123 of Chapter X of the Constitution, which reads: "The equality of the right of the citizens of the U.S.S.R. irrespective of their nationality or race, in all fields of economic, state, cultural, social, and political life, is an irrevocable law. Any direct or indirect restriction of these rights, or conversely the establishment of direct or indirect privileges for citizens on account of the race or nationality to which they belong, as well as the propagation of racial or national exceptionalism, or hatred and contempt, is punishable by law.

In 2017, while our current president appoints KKK members to the Department of Justice and calls Nazi murderers "very fine people," and his opponent in the 2016 elections, Hillary Clinton, called our children "super predators" and campaigned for them to be locked up en masse, we have to appreciate how significant it is that a national government — in 1919 — put laws on the books like ones described above. The Soviet Union outlawed racism. It invested heavily in Black education and Black artistic expression. The Soviets gave guns to those fighting imperialists and fascists all over the world. What more could you want? Terrell Jermaine Starr and The Root may be confused about which government cares about Black people, but I cannot say that I am. I am proud to be a socialist and I'm proud of the legacy of friendship between my people and the USSR.

As I mentioned in the start of this article, calling Africans who fight for their liberation "commies" or "dupes" is nothing new. John Hope Franklin referred to this in "From Slavery to Freedom," saying that the response to Black self-defense against race riots in 1919 caused such speculation: "Many American whites freely suggested that foreign influences — especially ... Bolshevik propaganda after the 1917 Russian Revolution — had caused [B]lacks to fight back. Perhaps there is some truth to that... However, [B]lack Americans all along the political spectrum (from conservative, to moderate, to radical left) ridiculed the claim that their new assertiveness was the result of 'outside agitation.' American [B]lacks needed no outsiders to awaken their sense of the tremendous contradiction between America's professed beliefs and its actual practices".

That remains as true today as when it was written. Additionally, I will close with one more statement from that time, which also remains true, at least for myself. The militant Black Harlem publication, "The Crusader," under the leadership of fiery Black Communist Cyril Briggs declared in 1919: "If to fight for one's rights is to be Bolshevists, then we are Bolshevists and let them make the most of it!" ☐

Directly from the library to the battlefield

How the ideas of 'The State and Revolution' changed history

BY BRIAN BECKER

This chapter originally appeared in "Revolution Manifesto: Understanding Marx and Lenin's Theory of Revolution" published by Liberation Media in 2015.

ANYONE who aspires to be a real communist or to understand the theory of modern communism must study Lenin's pamphlet "The State and Revolution."

Lenin was able to nearly finish this monumental contribution to Marxism and revolution while on the run, living underground and hiding from the police from August to October 1917, just before the insurrection that seized power.

"The State and Revolution" has been published in practically every written language. It is considered the veritable manifesto for the Russian Revolution. However, the book played no role in the revolution itself given that it was not published until after the workers had seized power in October/November 1917.[1]

The final version was written following the victorious October insurrection. If Lenin had written the book only as a guide to action for the revolution, it would have been unnecessary for him to devote so much time to finishing the book in the two months after the revolution. After all, at this time he and the other leading Bolsheviks were also confronted with the consuming crises and immediate life-and-death challenges facing the new government. The book's primary objective was not simply to serve as a guide to action for the unfolding events. Nor was it to describe what form a future socialist state would take. The book and its contents were written to re-establish the original revolutionary teachings of Marx on the need to smash and destroy the existing state power rather than using its parliamentary apparatus as the path to achieving socialism.

The book's primary objective was to rescue Marxism from its devolution into a doctrine of reform, to restore Marxism as a doctrine of revolution.

> *The book's primary objective was to rescue Marxism from its devolution into a doctrine of reform, to restore Marxism as a doctrine of revolution.*

Lenin writes in "The State and Revolution": "In view of the unprecedentedly widespread distortion of Marxism, our prime task is to re-establish what Marx really taught on the subject of the state."[2]

He accuses the leaders of the mass socialist parties of "doctoring" Marxism: "They omit, obliterate and distort the revolutionary side of this teaching, its revolutionary soul. They push to the foreground and extol [in Marx's writing] what is or seems acceptable to the bourgeoisie."

RESTUDYING MARX

The core ideas in "The State and Revolution" were developed by Lenin in January and February of 1917 and were based on his decision to restudy all that Marx and Engels had written on the question of state power.[3] This study took place in a library in Zurich, Switzerland, where Lenin was then in exile.

The core concepts were not developed in response to the prospects, possibilities and challenges of the rapidly unfolding revolutionary process that began in February 1917 and culminated with the Bolshevik-led insurrection in October. Rather, they were developed in response to an ongoing theoretical debate between Karl Kautsky, widely recognized as the leading Marxist theoretician of the international socialist movement, and "left" Marxists.[4]

The question of how the socialists could win political power, and whether the existing state power in capitalist society could be used as an instrument in building socialism, had evolved in a steadily less revolutionary direction since the death of Marx in 1883. Given that the capitalist states had plunged the world into a war of unprecedented destruction, this theoretical dispute was no idle matter but had pressing and immense significance for the general strategy of socialists everywhere.

In this context, Lenin decided to restudy Marx and Engels, and this led him to change or sharpen his own view on the subject.[5]

Although not published until January 1918, the ideas expressed in the book played a fundamental role months earlier in the success of the first socialist seizure of power. Lenin had transmitted the revolutionary essence of these ideas to the Bolshevik leaders, and from there, these ideas guided the party as a whole. Simply put, the October socialist revolution could not have succeeded without the party's leadership, and that leadership would have been impossible had the party not been inculcated with the ideas Lenin developed on the question of the state.

TAKING ON KAUTSKY'S THEORETICAL LEADERSHIP

The book's central ideas represented a sharp departure from the mainstream socialist parties that had become a significant force in Germany and other European parliaments. They also constituted a shift in the thinking of the Bolshevik Party.

"The State and Revolution" was a polemic directed against the core leadership of the parties of the Socialist International (also known as the Second International), and especially against Karl Kautsky and the German Social-Democratic Party, the flagship of international socialism at that time. The mainstream of the socialist movement had forgotten, or chosen to ignore, the conclusions that Marx and Engels developed about the state following the experience of two failed revolutions: the February 1848 revolutions in France and Germany, and, of even greater consequence, the Paris Commune of 1871. In 1871, tens of thousands of Parisian workers were slaughtered and their Commune destroyed following a two-month hold on political power.

Lenin makes clear the primary task of the book in its very first sentences:

> What is now happening to Marx's teachings has, in the course of history, happened repeatedly to the teachings of revolutionary thinkers and leaders of oppressed classes

struggling for emancipation. During the lifetime of great revolutionaries, the oppressing classes constantly hounded them, received their teachings with the most savage malice, the most furious hatred and the most unscrupulous campaigns of lies and slander. After their death, attempts are made to convert them into harmless icons, to canonize them, so to say, and to surround their *names* with a certain halo for the 'consolation' of the oppressed classes and with the object of duping the latter, while at the same time emasculating the *essence* of the revolutionary teaching, blunting its revolutionary edge and vulgarizing it.[6]

THE EVOLUTION OF MARX AND ENGELS' VIEWS ON REVOLUTION AND THE STATE

Marx and Engels approached political theory as a science. Their theory was based on an examination of facts, evidence, data and experience. They did not engage in much speculation about the future. They did not dream up utopias, schemes or new systems for a better world. Their theory was based on the generalized experience of the class struggle in history.

> *Marx and Engels approached political theory as a science. Their theory was based on an examination of facts, evidence, data and experience.*

The "Communist Manifesto" was written on the eve of profound (bourgeois) democratic revolutions that swept France, Germany and other countries in Europe in 1848. Those revolutions ended in violent defeats in 1849 for what Marx and Engels termed the democratic party (representing the peasantry and urban middle classes) and the workers' party (representing the working class). The result was fierce repression of working-class activists for decades to come. Marx and Engels were forced to flee Germany and spent the rest of their lives in exile in England.

In France, as a result of an economic crisis that began in England in 1847 and spread to France, a coalition government came to power in February 1848 following the collapse of the regime of King Louis Philippe. The new government promised unemployed workers a job, among other reforms.

In June 1848, the French government moved to close down these economic reforms, and the workers alone defended them against both the big and petty bourgeoisie. Though ending in defeat after a valiant struggle, this was the first time in France that the working class acted politically as an independent force and not as the tail of the radical democratic petty bourgeoisie.

'WINNING THE BATTLE OF DEMOCRACY'

The "Communist Manifesto" had argued that the proletariat must end the political supremacy of the capitalists by attaining or achieving political power, and the state power must be radically altered into the "proletariat organized as the ruling class" and by the working class "winning the battle of democracy."

But the Manifesto had not answered the question of how this task was to be accomplished.

Only the defeats of the revolutions in 1848 allowed Marx to go beyond the Manifesto's general formula and sum up that experience with greater clarity. Studying the 1848 revolutions, he could deal with the question of state power in a specific, particular way, rather than with an abstract formula. In 1852, Marx wrote: "All [earlier] revolutions perfected this machine instead of smashing it."[7] He declared that the proletarian revolution must break up and destroy the state machine.

Marx and Engels considered this conclusion to be an important step forward in their theory of revolution, and foundational to their entire world outlook by 1852.

In an 1852 letter to a follower living in the United States, Marx wrote:

> And now as to myself, no credit is due to me for discovering the existence of classes in modern society, nor yet the struggle between them. Long before me bourgeois historians have described the historical development of the struggle of the classes and bourgeois economists the economic anatomy of the classes. What I did that was new was to prove: 1) that the existence of classes is only bound up with particular historical phases in the development of production; 2) that the class struggle necessarily

leads to the dictatorship of the proletariat; 3) that the dictatorship itself only constitutes the transition to the abolition of all classes into a classless society.[8]

Marx did not speculate about what form a future workers' state might take. He was not in the business of providing prophesies about what the future "better world" would look like nor what form the "dictatorship of the proletariat" would take. The history of the class struggle had not yet answered that question of what could and would take the place of the smashed and broken up state power.

LEARNING FROM THE PARIS COMMUNE

Only the seizure and holding of political power for two months by the working class in Paris in 1871 — the Paris Commune — presented the experience and evidence of what a workers' state would look like and its fundamental difference from the bourgeois state.

The "Communist Manifesto" "has in some details become antiquated," wrote Marx and Engels in 1872, "in view of the practical experience gained, first in the [1848] February Revolution, and then, still more, in the Paris Commune, where the proletariat for the first time held political power for two whole months. ... One thing especially was proved by the Commune, viz., that 'the working class cannot simply lay hold of the ready-made state machinery, and wield it for its own purposes.' "[9]

Marx died 12 years after the Paris Commune. The defeat of the Paris Commune set the movement back, and the First International splintered in its wake. Marx and Engels moved its headquarters from London to New York City, where it contracted further and died a few years later.[10]

There was widespread despair, a mood that accompanies every big setback for the movement. But within a few years a revival began, although in much less revolutionary form. In the decade after Marx's death, Engels functioned as the advisor and consultant to the socialist movements in Europe.[11] As the industrial revolution spread rapidly in the years following the Paris Commune, the workers' struggle changed in form, magnitude and tone. The tempestuous growth of organized labor unions coincided with the expansion of the right to vote. While the Communards in Paris had "stormed the heavens" in raging street fighting, the new socialist movement was channeled into mass union organizing and electoral politics. Socialist parties based in the working class grew exponentially.

Less revolutionary than the Paris Commune but wider in scope, the new socialist parties formed a Second International. Although Marx functioned as an organizational leader of the First International, which did not yet include socialist parties but groups and movements, his ideological and political followers were only a small minority. The Second International by contrast was based on new political parties that possessed a mass base within the working class, and they all identified as Marxists.

Thus the teachings of Marx and Engels became the dominant political force within the Second International. The new international was a huge step forward for Marxism, socialism and the workers' struggle. But as the new workers' parties of the Second International expanded their influence by organizing large trade unions and winning elections in the parliamentary arena, they blunted Marxism's revolutionary essence.

ATTITUDE OF THE GERMAN SOCIAL DEMOCRATIC PARTY AFTER THE DEATH OF MARX

By the early 20th century, the right to vote — for propertyless male workers — had been achieved in large parts of Europe. Mass socialist parties representing the working classes gained ever larger blocs of seats within the parliaments of various countries.

These parties were led by people who considered themselves Marxists and had come to believe that parliamentary struggle was the way to win the "conquest of political power" by the proletariat.

The most important socialist party in Europe was the German Social Democratic Party (SPD). This party and its theoretical leaders, including Karl Kautsky, were considered the "center" of the Socialist International. Lenin, too, recognized the leadership of the SPD and Kautsky until August 1914, when the SPD delegates in the Reichstag (the German parliament) voted to support the German war effort with the outbreak of WWI.

Kautsky, who was considered by many an orthodox Marxist but actually had become a centrist (revolutionary in words, reformist in deeds), clearly envisioned that the "conquest of political power," as described in the "Communist Manifesto" could be secured through a peaceful, parliamentary path. By gaining the majority in parliament and raising the socialist-led parliament to be the directing force of government, the SPD could chart a path for the socialist reorganization of the economy.

"The goal of our political struggle remains the same as it has been up to now: the conquest of state power through winning a majority in the parliament and raising parliament to be the master of government. Not, however, the destruction of state power," wrote Karl Kautsky in 1912.[12]

For today's reader, it is critically important to understand why this prospect of a peaceful transition to socialism in Germany seemed plausible at the time, rather than just a dream.

Germany had anti-socialist laws in place until 1890. Thus, the Social Democratic Party, which had been formed in 1875, had to work under conditions of illegality. When those laws were lifted and the party could function legally, it grew rapidly.

By 1910, the SPD was the most vibrant force in German society. For one, SPD organizers were dominant in the German labor unions. The party published newspapers, magazines, pamphlets and books; it created musical and choir organizations; it established organized networks of worker-poets; it established 125 local children's organizations and 574 youth organizations to provide education, culture and recreational activities for young people; it established a "free advice" program in most cities that provided advice to help working people secure legal and

Karl Kautsky, major Marxist theoritician, leader of the non-revolutionary wing of German Social Democracy

economic benefits from the state; it had its own beer halls where working people gathered.

By 1912, the SPD had grown to nearly a million members. It had in some ways developed a socialist-led "state within the state."[13] SPD leaders and members envisioned an electoral success that would give a mandate for this "state within the state" to be extended nationwide as the new model.

In the 1912 parliamentary elections, the SPD won the largest number of votes of any party, and became the largest bloc within the Reichstag, with 110 seats. Based on this success, the SPD became the "model" for all socialist parties at that time.[14]

But it was precisely because it was so successful as a legal party that its leaders did not want to "lose everything" that they had achieved. When WWI broke out between the competing capitalist governments of Europe, the SPD was forced to decide how its delegates would vote inside parliament. To vote against the expenditures needed for war (war credits) would have had the party labeled as traitors by the German army's high command.

This charge of treason would undoubtedly have also been made by many of the millions of workers who had voted for the SPD. As happens in the beginning of all major wars, a war hysteria swept the population. The threat of annihilation from the "enemy," in this case the reactionary armies of the Russian monarchy, created a wave of patriotism and national unity. To vote against the war funds in this context would have meant standing against this wave and facing the allegation of helping tsarist Russia.

The SPD leadership, along with the other parties in the Socialist International, had seen ahead of time that the danger of a world war was real. In 1912, all the socialist parties had met at a conference in Basel, Switzerland, and vowed that if war came each national party would oppose the workers of their country being sent to kill and be killed by workers from other countries.[15] At the conference, they raised again the banner of the "Communist Manifesto": workers of the world, unite!

On the eve of war, the Manifesto of the Basel Congress called out: "The Congress therefore appeals to you, proletarians and socialists of all countries, to make your voices heard in this decisive hour! Proclaim your will in every form and in all places; raise your protest in the parliaments with all your force; unite in great mass demonstrations. ..."[16]

But then, in August 1914, the war broke out. With the impe-

> 'The Congress therefore appeals to you, proletarians and socialists of all countries, to make your voices heard in this decisive hour!'

rialist powers attacking and invading each other, would the socialists stand aside and oppose their country's armies who were in a life-and-death battle to "save" their nation? To do so certainly meant losing legal status. It meant having mass organizations closed down and their members in parliament sent to prison for treason.

The Russian Social Democratic Labor Party faced the same challenge in August 1914. The Bolshevik faction of the party had won the seats set aside for working-class districts in the parliament (the Duma). Under Lenin's direction, they voted against the war credits. [17] They adhered to the resolution of the Basel Congress. They were imprisoned and indicted as traitors to Russia and went to trial facing the death penalty if convicted.

In Germany, 109 out of the SPD's 110 parliamentary delegates voted for war credits. Karl Liebknecht, a member of the left wing of the SPD, abstained (as had been recommended by Kautsky) but voted "No" on a subsequent resolution. In spite of his parliamentary immunity, Liebknecht was arrested, drafted into the army and dispatched to the Eastern Front of the war against Russia.

THE EVOLUTION OF LENIN'S VIEW OF THE STATE

Lenin's "The State and Revolution" broke with the thinking of the majority of the socialist parties.

Until the outbreak of WWI and the capitulation of the German socialists to the war effort, Lenin had accepted Kautsky as the leading Marxist theoretician of the international movement.

He had not challenged the dominant views of other Marxists on the question of the state. He had denounced Kautsky as a traitor to socialism because of his position on the war in 1914, but before 1917 he had not challenged Kautsky's view on the state.

Biographers and scholars on Lenin have different views of whether "The State and Revolution" was a transformative work that led Lenin to rethink his own views on the subject.[18] He certainly did not, of course, share Kautsky's infatuation with the parliamentary road to socialism. Lenin, for instance, had supported the launching of an armed struggle during the 1905 Russian Revolution.

But prior to 1917, Lenin did not enter the theoretical debate between Kautsky and "left-wing" Marxists on the role of the

Karl Liebknecht and Rosa Luxemburg, leaders of the revolutionary wing of German Social Democracy

state and how the socialists could achieve political power.

In 1916, Dutch Marxist Anton Pannekoek and later Russian Nicholai Bukharin published "leftist" criticisms of Kautsky's position on the state.

Pannekoek argued that the socialist movement and the cause of the working class "is not simply a struggle with the bourgeoisie over state power as an object, but a struggle against state power."[19]

Kautsky responded, as quoted earlier, that a socialist-led government could and should become "the master of government," but with the aim of using, and not destroying, the state power.

In a 1916 article, Bukharin argued along the same lines as Pannekoek that a new socialist society led by an empowered working class must "outgrow the framework of the state and burst it from within as they organize their own state power" or else the new socialist power would eventually be absorbed by the capitalist state structures. Lenin rejected the article for publication.

Lenin decided to directly participate in the debate between Kautsky and the "left" Marxists in December 1916. His remarks at that point suggest that he considered Kautsky's views closer to the position of orthodox Marxism than Bukharin's:

Socialists are in favor of using the present state and its institutions in the struggle for the emancipation of the working class, maintaining also that the state should be used for a specific form of transition from capitalism to socialism. This transitional form is the dictatorship of the proletariat, which is *also* a state. The anarchists want to 'abolish' the state, 'blow it up' as Comrade Nota-Bena (Bukharin) expresses it one place, erroneously ascribing this view to the socialists.[20]

In a review of this debate, political scientist Marian Sawer has argued that Lenin's three months devoted to the restudying of Marx and Engels' position on the state was what led to a dramatic change in his own position on the state. As a consequence, she says, Lenin came closer to Bukharin's orientation but then went far beyond anything written by the "left" Marxists in developing a comprehensive position on the need to smash the bourgeois state and replace it with a state of a new type: the commune state.

For the first time, Lenin writes of the worker and peasant soviets (popular councils), which had been created spontaneously from below during the 1905 revolution, as the embryo of a new alternative state power to the capitalist state.

The timing of Lenin's theoretical study on the Marxist view of revolution coincided accidentally with the outbreak of a real revolution. All of the freshly thought-through ideas about the need to smash the state and create a new state power immediately became applicable in life.

With the outbreak of the revolution, all of Lenin's attention switched to finding a way back to Russia without being murdered or jailed along the way. Lenin feared that his notes on Marx and Engels' writings on the state — what became famously known as the Blue Notebook — could be confiscated on the trip back from Zurich. The notebook was left behind and he was only able to retrieve it later through Sweden. But even without the notes in hand, Lenin was crystal clear on the task at hand.

Even before securing safe passage back to Russia from exile, he wrote: "Thus the St. Petersburg workers, having overthrown the tsarist monarchy, immediately set up their *own* organization, the Soviet of Workers' Deputies, immediately proceeded to strengthen and extend it, to organize independent Soviets of Workers and Soldiers' Deputies. Only a few days after the revolution, the St. Petersburg Soviet of Workers and Soldiers' Deputies comprised over 1,500 deputies of workers and peasants dressed in soldier's uniforms. It enjoyed such wide confidence among railway workers and the entire mass of the laboring population that it began to develop into a real *people's government.*"[22]

CHANGING THE BOLSHEVIK ORIENTATION

Lenin arrived in Russia on April 3, 1917. When he first presented his worked-out thoughts on the state and its practical implications, they sent a shock wave through both the Bolshevik and Menshevik leaderships. Lenin read his "April Theses" out loud to a gathering of Bolshevik leaders on April 4. In fact, he did so twice so that the meaning of his proposals could be fully understood. The next day, he read them to a meeting of both Bolshevik and Menshevik leaders.

The "April Theses" represented a major reorientation. Lenin called for the overthrow of the newly created "Provisional" capitalist coalition government that had arisen after the February Revolution and the replacement of this existing state power with a new state power led by grassroots Workers' and Peasants' Councils (Soviets). He invoked the Paris Commune in the "April Theses", although

The Petrograd Soviet

PHOTO: EVERETT HISTORICAL

without much explanation, and insisted that the comrades reread what Marx wrote about the Commune in 1871, 1872 and 1875.[23]

Both the moderate, Menshevik faction of the Social Democratic Labor Party of Russia and the revolutionary faction of the Bolsheviks rejected Lenin's position. Upon hearing his "April Theses" at their meeting, the St. Petersburg Committee voted 13-2 to reject the position Lenin offered. The Bolshevik Committee in Moscow also voted to reject the Theses.

Almost all the other Bolshevik leaders were supporting, although in a critical way, the Provisional coalition government that had replaced the fallen czar in the February Revolution (1917). That new government was dominated by the bourgeois-liberal Cadet Party, the peasant-based Socialist Revolutionaries and the Mensheviks. The Bolsheviks were offering critical support while attempting to push it to the left.

The "April Theses" and the struggle it provoked inside the Bolshevik Party has been examined and re-examined by socialists and scholars of the Russian Revolution and in all the biographies on Lenin.

THE CLASS CHARACTER OF THE REVOLUTION

Most of these discussions center on just one side of an internal controversy that had been debated for more than a decade but was brought into sharper focus by the "April Theses": the class character of the coming revolution.

This was the question of whether the upcoming revolution in Russia, which all sides agreed would fundamentally be a bourgeois-democratic revolution, would be led by the liberal bourgeoisie (the Menshevik position) or by the "democratic dictatorship" of the workers and the peasantry as a whole (the position put forward by Lenin in 1905 and adopted by the Bolsheviks).

According to this formula, Lenin foresaw an alliance between, on the one side, the peasantry including the kulaks (capitalist farmers), middle and small-holding peasants and the landless poor that would neutralize the big bourgeoisie and, on the other side, the working class through the Russian Social Democratic Labor Party, which could play the leading role politically since it would see the way forward that no peasant party possibly could.

Most of the Bolshevik leaders, therefore, believed that Marxists could enter a revolutionary government together with the democratic petty bourgeoisie, even if the workers' party did not rule outright. Rather, the workers' party would play the role of ensuring the best political conditions — a democratic republic — for capitalist development to replace feudalism, and for the workers' struggle against the capitalists.

The implication of Lenin's formula of a "democratic dictatorship" was that the bourgeoisie in Russia was too enfeebled, too tied to the feudal landowners and imperialism, and too unrevolutionary to carry out radical land reform and other measures enacted by the bourgeois revolutions in Europe a century or more earlier. In other words, Lenin's formula of the "democratic dictatorship of the workers and peasantry" anticipated a bourgeois-democratic revolution but without the bourgeoisie or its political parties leading the fight.

> *[Lenin] anticipated a bourgeois-democratic revolution but without the bourgeoisie or its political parties leading the fight.*

When Lenin insisted in April 1917 that the Bolsheviks withdraw support for the Provisional government and instead call for all power to the Soviets, some Bolsheviks argued that Lenin had abandoned his own theory about the bourgeois-democratic stage of the Russian Revolution. They asked how it could be that Russia, if it first required a bourgeois-democratic revolution (against feudalism and its remnants), later followed by a socialist revolution, would only need a bourgeois-democratic revolution as a historical stage that lasted two months?

Lenin would not have considered the "April Theses" conclusions to be an abandonment of the earlier formula regarding the democratic dictatorship of the workers and peasantry.

He had written two years earlier (October 1915) that this democratic dictatorship would closely connect the bourgeois-democratic revolution and the socialist revolution. "The task confronting the proletariat in Russia is the consummation of the bourgeois-democratic revolution in Russia *in order* to kindle the socialist revolution in Europe."[24]

The second point in the Theses stated: "The specific feature of the present situation in Russia is that the country is *passing* from the first stage of the revolution — which, owing to the insufficient class-consciousness and organization of the proletariat, placed power in the hands of the bourgeoisie — to its *second stage*, which must place power in the hands of the proletariat and the poorest sections of the peasants."[25]

The Theses' seventh point called for: "The immediate union of all banks in the country into a single national bank, and the institution of control over it by the Soviet of Workers' Deputies." This "transitional demand" suggests that Lenin believed at that point in the revolution that the country, in spite of its economic and social/cultural backwardness, could move in the direction of socialism — though not necessarily to socialism itself. Many bourgeois-democratic revolutions in economically backward countries have carried out nationalizations of banks and major industries to advance the development of capitalism, not socialism.

In the eighth point, Lenin makes this clear: "It is not our *immediate* task to 'introduce' socialism, but only to bring social production and the distribution of products at once under the *control* of the Soviets of Workers' Deputies." (Lenin's emphasis). In light of the horrific destruction and social agony of WWI and its potentially revolutionary consequences not just in Russia but in the advanced capitalist countries as well, Lenin was at this point leaving somewhat open the actual near-term course of the Russian revolution.

But Lenin had already come to the conclusion that the second revolution that he was now advocating as an imminent, short-term prospect — not as an event for the distant future — would be the inauguration of the international socialist revolution. This was so even though Russia was still devoid of the material prerequisites to finish the construction of socialism.

His nuanced views on this were succinctly explained in his "Farewell Letter to the Swiss Workers," written on March 26, just eight days before he returned to Russia and read his "April Theses" to his startled comrades:

> However, it was not our impatience, nor our wishes, but the *objective conditions* created by the imperialist war that brought the *whole of* humanity to an impasse, that placed it in a dilemma: either allow the destruction of more millions of lives and utterly ruin European civilisation, or hand over power in *all* the civilised countries to the revolutionary proletariat, carry through the socialist revolution.

To the Russian proletariat has fallen the great honour of beginning the series of revolutions which the imperialist war has made an objective inevitability. But the idea that the Russian proletariat is the chosen revolutionary proletariat among the workers of the world is absolutely alien to us. We know perfectly well that the proletariat of Russia is less organised, less prepared and less class-conscious than the proletariat of other countries. It is not its special qualities, but rather the special conjuncture of historical circumstances that *for a certain, perhaps very short,* time has made the proletariat of Russia the vanguard of the revolutionary proletariat of the whole world.

Russia is a peasant country, one of the most backward of European countries. Socialism *cannot* triumph there *directly* and *immediately.* But the peasant character of the country, the vast reserve of land in the hands of the nobility, *may,* to judge from the experience of 1905, give tremendous sweep to the bourgeois-democratic revolution in Russia and *may* make our revolution the prologue to the world socialist revolution, a *step* toward it. ...

In Russia, socialism cannot triumph directly and immediately. But the peasant mass *can* bring the inevitable and matured agrarian upheaval to the point of *confiscating* all the immense holdings of the nobility. ...

Such a revolution would not, in itself, be socialism. But it would give a great impetus to the world labour movement. It would immensely strengthen the position of the socialist proletariat in Russia and its influence on the agricultural labourers and the poorest peasants. It would enable the city proletariat to develop, on the strength of this influence, such revolutionary organisations as the Soviets of Workers' Deputies to replace the old instruments of oppression employed by bourgeois states, the army, the police, the bureaucracy; to carry out — under pressure of the unbearably burdensome imperialist war

and its consequences — a series of revolutionary measures to *control* the production and distribution of goods.

> Single-handed, the Russian proletariat cannot bring
> the socialist revolution to a *victorious conclusion*. But
> it can give the Russian revolution a mighty sweep that
> would create the most favourable conditions for a socialist
> revolution, and would, in a sense, start it. It can facil-
> itate the rise of a situation in which its *chief,* its most
> trustworthy and most reliable collaborator, the *European*
> and American *socialist* proletariat, could join the decisive
> battles. (Lenin's emphasis)

SMASHING AND REPLACING THE EXISTING STATE

Lenin's strategic reorientation of the Party and the controversy
it created inside the Bolsheviks has been the subject of widespread
attention and examination.

But the other side to the "April Theses" debate has been given less
attention. Lenin's thinking had evolved and had now gone much further
than others in the socialist and Marxist movement in his insistence on
the need to smash, break up the state and replace it with a new one —
a power such as that created by the short-lived Paris Commune.

By raising the Soviets as an alternative state power, a new
historical iteration of the commune state, Lenin was arguing that
these spontaneously created and democratically elected councils of
workers', soldiers' and peasants' deputies could not only defend the
people's interests and the struggle for democracy but also could function as a new state power. Instead of utilizing the existing state power
for socialist ends, the existing state could be broken up, smashed and
replaced with a new state based on another class power.

In the 1905 revolution, where soviets had first appeared as a grassroots innovation, Lenin had portrayed the soviets as a kind of united
front rather than an embryonic new state power: "The Soviet of Workers'
Deputies is not a labor parliament and an organ of self-government at all,
but a fighting organization for the achievement of definite aims."

The core argument of the "April Theses" was more ambitious:
Lenin was, in effect, proposing the smashing of the existing state and
creating an entirely new and fundamentally different type of state.

In Lenin's notebook from the restudy of Marx and Engels' works, it is clear that he re-evaluated the role of the Soviets as the basis for a Commune-type state along the lines of what was created in Paris in 1871 and which Marx analyzed with great detail. That process of examining the experience of the commune had, as stated above, also sharpened Marx's own view on the question of the state and revolution.[26]

This theoretical study not only sharpened Lenin's views. They were literally brought by him from the library to the battlefield of the revolution itself.

Lenin did not favor calling for the immediate overthrow of the Provisional government by the Soviets. Because the majority of workers and poor peasants were still following and supporting the bourgeois-led Provisional revolutionary government:

> We must explain to the masses that the Soviet of Workers Deputies is the only possible form of revolutionary government; and that, therefore, our task is, while this [Soviet] government is submitting to the influence of the bourgeoisie, a patient, systematic and persistent explanation to the masses the error of their tactics.[27]

Lenin believed that the unwillingness of the Provisional government to end Russia's involvement in WWI would lead the workers, based on their own living experience, to come over to the Bolsheviks' attitude about the need for a revolutionary insurrection.

Lenin's authority within the organization and his unmatched respect allowed him to win over the majority of his opponents within a few days. The Bolsheviks reoriented and were on the path to revolution, which they accomplished seven months later.

Lenin's presentation of the "April Theses" was followed by numerous articles, letters and speeches by him during the subsequent months of revolution, setback, repression, renewal and finally the seizure of power. The themes and ideas from April were repeated and re-explained as the tide of events took sharp and unexpected turns.

Beginning in July 1917, after the Mensheviks and Socialist Revolutionaries — who had the majority of delegates in the Soviet — had insisted on continuing the war and had refused to respond to the

Pro-war Russian poster issued in 1917, before the October Revolution.

demands of the peasants for land, the Bolsheviks even temporarily withdrew for a time their call for all power to the soviets.

This was to avoid the potential misperception among the increasingly restive and radicalized workers that the Bolsheviks call for Soviet power could be interpreted as support for the continuation of the war or that they would turn their backs on the poor peasants who were bent on seizing the lands of the nobility and large landlords.

As the bourgeois-led Provisional government caved to the pressure of Britain, France and the United States to continue the war, the moderate socialists who joined the Provisional government lost credibility among the workers. By September, the tactic of "persistent and patient" explanation about the inadequacies of the Provisional government showed its correctness as public opinion shifted dramatically to the left and the Bolshevik delegates became the elected majority of the Soviets.

Once they had majority support in the Soviets, Lenin insisted that preparations for an insurrection begin. On October 25 (November 7), the Bolshevik-led insurrection brought the Soviets to power. Their political support had become so widespread that the revolution was nearly bloodless.

Lenin emerged from hiding on the day of victory. He spoke briefly to the Meeting of the Petrograd Soviet of Workers' and Soldiers' Deputies and offered a resolution. These brief remarks summarize with complete clarity Lenin's theses on the character of the state and the revolution which created it:

What is the significance of the workers' and peasants' revolution? Its significance is, first of all, that we shall have a Soviet government, our own organ of power, in which the bourgeoisie will have no share whatsoever. The oppressed masses will themselves create a power. The old state apparatus will be shattered to its foundations and a new administrative apparatus set up in the form of Soviet organizations.[28]

Was the new Soviet power, the new workers' and peasants' government, to be a socialist or a bourgeois-democratic regime? Lenin was as clear as day. The two stages of revolution had become intertwined as a consequence of the international situation. "From now on, a new phase in the history of Russia begins, and this, the third Russian Revolution, should in the end lead to the victory of socialism." He announced the trajectory: "We possess the strength of mass organization, which will overcome everything and lead the proletariat to the world revolution." He ended: "We must now set about building a proletarian socialist state in Russia. Long live the world socialist revolution!"

Lenin's concepts and views on the question of the state and revolution were finally presented in their fullness with the publication of "The State and Revolution" two months later.

SUMMARY

Because its topic is not limited to Russia but to the tasks facing all modern revolutions that seek to overturn power in bourgeois society, and because Lenin and the Bolsheviks actually succeeded in making the revolution in 1917, "The State and Revolution" was embraced in the early 1920s by the international communist movement as a guiding document for the revolutionary struggles of the working class.

Left-wing socialists and pro-communist anarchists united and formed new communist parties to challenge the reformist socialist parties. They were inspired by the Russian Revolution, and "The State and Revolution" became their new manifesto of the 20th century.

But just as Marx and Engels' writings on the state were "forgotten" by the Marxist leaders of the socialist parties and just as these founders of scientific socialism were "converted into harmless icons" and the essence of their revolutionary teachings blunted and vulgarized, so too were the works of Lenin by many of the Marxists who came later.

This was a complicated historical process and went through various stages stretching over several decades. First the victories of Nazism and fascism in Germany, Italy and Spain — and then the spread of fascism throughout continental Europe — not only crushed both the communist and socialist parties but caused a re-orientation away from proletarian revolution in Europe.

The PSL anticipates that the current global contradictions emanating from imperialism and the repeated economic crises of capitalism will lead to a new wave of revolutionary mobilization.

Instead of smashing the state and making revolution, most of the communist movement in Europe retreated in its strategy and objectives. The main goal in the short term was to "preserve democracy" and prevent the capture of state power by fascist organizations. Preserving democracy, they thought, meant allying with the liberal bourgeoisie to preserve rather than smash the existing state.

Assigning this non-revolutionary task to the communist movement required a "reinterpretation" of Lenin's key writings. Since these parties declared themselves to be Marxist-Leninists, it required them, to reinterpret the meaning of Marx and Lenin's foundational texts or ignore their applicability. They had to essentially pretend that they did not exist or have relevance in the modern world. This was precisely how the Second International reformist socialists had vulgarized Marx's view of the state.

The PSL anticipates that the current global contradictions emanating from imperialism and the repeated economic crises of capitalism will lead to a new wave of revolutionary mobilization and the revival of socialism as the only counterpoint to capitalism. That is why we are republishing and restudying "The State and Revolution."

Each new generation of working-class activists and fighters needs to read and study this manifesto of revolution, which restored the essence of Marx's prescription about how to build a better world. □

The actuality of revolution

BY JODI DEAN

REVOLUTION today names more a problem than it does a solu-tion. We know that revolutions happen, but we have a hard time believing in revolution. We have a hard time believing in revolution because we are no longer confident that the revolutionary process leads in an emancipatory egalitarian direction. There are revolutions, but they are not for us, not the revolutions we were hoping for, not proletarian revolutions.

We no longer believe in revolution because we no longer adopt the perspective from which we see ourselves as revolutionaries, the perspective of the communist party. Absent this political perspective, only capitalism with its permanent crises, innovations and transfor-mations appears as capable of effecting revolutionary change. Fortu-nately, the crowds and demonstrations of the last decade suggest that a new party perspective may be emerging. The collective practices and intensities exhibited in current struggles, as well as the limits against which these struggles falter, are renewing the salience of the party question on the Left. As people experience their collective power, the desire for something like a party is reemerging, a party as the organized site of our belief in revolution.

In this essay I focus on two, seemingly opposed, approaches to organization and revolution. I begin with Georg Lukács's account of the Leninist innovation: the realization that the core of historical materialism is the actuality of the proletarian revolution. The force of this innovation comes from *anticipation*, the capacity of the future revolution to coordinate the actions that will bring it about. I then turn to the present and the work of Michael Hardt and Antonio Negri. The problem with their account is that it precludes the temporality that would produce revolutionary practice. Revolution is present as *potential*, a possibility that flows out of what we are already doing. There is no revolutionary break, no negation of some practices, trajectories, and potentials in the forwarding of emancipatory egalitarian aims. Theirs is thus a "revolution without revolution." In contrast, the future projected in Lenin's assumption of the actuality of revolution coordinates political action to bring revolution into being. The party anticipates the revolution, materializing the belief that makes revolution possible not just as an outflow or overflow of present possibilities, but as an effect of the negation of some practices, trajectories, and potentials and the forcing of others.

> *'Every revolution seems impossible at the beginning, and after it happens, it was inevitable.'*
> — Bill Ayers

My argument relies on Jean-Pierre Dupuy's notion of "projected time." Dupuy introduces "projected time" as a name for "coordination by means of the future," that is, as a term for a temporal metaphysics wherein "the future counterfactually determines the past, which in turn causally determines it. The future is fixed, but its necessity exists only in retrospect."[1] From the perspective of the future, what led to it was necessary. It could not have been otherwise because everything that happened led to it. Before an event occurs, there are possibilities, options. After something happens, it appears inevitable, destined. Projected time assumes a future inevitability, establishing this inevitability as the fixed point from which to decide upon present actions.

Projected time might seem strange. Dupuy explains that it is actually "the temporality peculiar to someone who carries out a plan that he has given to himself to carry out."[2] Planning makes clear how projected time is not a prediction of what will happen, a fantasy about what one wants to happen, or a set of proposals regarding what should happen.[3] Instead, a certain outcome generates the processes that lead to it. Again, in this temporal metaphysics, the future is not the inevitable effect of a chain of causes. The future is itself the cause. The future produces the past that will give rise to it.

Dupuy developed the metaphysics of projected time in the context of an investigation of catastrophe. People have a hard time believing in imminent disaster, even in the face of abundant information that the worst is about to happen. Dupuy concluded that the obstacle preventing people from acting is not one of knowledge but one of belief. They know what will happen, nevertheless they do not believe that it will happen. Projected time addresses this level of belief. Dupuy wagers that since it is "more difficult to reject a fate than to avoid a calamity, the threat of catastrophe becomes far more credible if it appears to be something that is inevitable."[4] That very inevitability can mobilize the determination and imagination necessary for avoiding the inevitable.

A VIEW FROM THE FUTURE

"Lenin: A Study on the Unity of His Thought" is Lukács' account of the enormity of Lenin's theoretical contribution: Lenin realized Marxist theory in practice. Because he grasps "the actuality of the revolution," Lenin can explain the events around him in its terms. He posits a certain future — the revolution — and lets this future guide action in the present. Lenin thus identifies the mechanism through which organization mediates between theory and practice. The projected future of revolution generates the practices that materialize the belief necessary for its realization.

Projected time tells us how to read Lukács's claim that "the proletarian revolution constitutes the living core of Marxism."[5] The revolutionary future determines the actions that bring it about. Historical materialism is not primarily an account of the past. It is a relation to a specific future, one where *revolution is already on its agenda.*"[6] A distant future lacks coordinating capacity. Lenin, however, made the actuality of revolution into the point from which actions are considered. This certain future enables choices and decisions. It cuts through the manifold conflicts of groups and individuals within the masses, as well as the economic fatalism that contributes to capitalism's own response to crises.

The actuality of revolution is the presupposition on which Lenin's concept of the party rests. The projected future of proletarian revolution causes the Bolsheviks to select "single-minded revolutionaries, prepared to make any sacrifice, from the more or less chaotic mass of the class as a whole." The party does not make the revolution. Nor does it try to pull along inactive masses and present them with a *fait accompli.* Instead, it anticipates the revolution. Given that the period is revolutionary, that the proletarian revolution is on the agenda, what form of organization follows? Lenin's answer is the "strictest selection of party members on the basis of their proletarian class-consciousness, and total solidarity with and support for all the oppressed and exploited within capitalist society."[7] Why? Because of the way the proletariat develops its own class-consciousness and becomes able to put it to use in the context of revolutionary upheaval.

In the course of its revolutionary movement, the proletariat encounters differences within and without it. The internal differences involve economic differentiation within the proletariat (the infamous "labor aristocracy"). The external differences refer to the other-classes part of the revolutionary alliance. Differences within the proletariat hinder class unity. Some workers, perhaps those with more education or experience in union leadership, tend to see their interests as allied with the bourgeoisie. Differences between the proletariat and other social strata create confusion, particularly as crises intensify and the revolutionary period gets nearer. The multiplicity of interests within the revolutionary alliance of the oppressed pulls them in different directions. Not every potential present in the masses forwards the

This Soviet poster, issued for the fifth anniversary of the Bolshevik Revolution, embodies the revolutionary optimism of the Leninist party

revolution. Figuring out the correct path, and keeping together the alliance through which all can win, becomes increasingly difficult.

Lenin's model of the party responds to the pull of these differences by providing an independent organizational space for the "fully conscious elements of the proletariat." Lukács writes, "It is this that demonstrates *that the Leninist form of organization is inseparably connected with the ability to foresee the approaching revolution.*"[8] In the party, even the most seemingly trivial decision becomes significant, that is, made in light of the projected future of proletarian revolution. A party decision cuts through myriad possibilities, directing action in one way rather than another.

Lukács's account makes clear that even as this view of the future provides the party with its organizational form, it is the party that sustains the view. He addresses the debate between Kautsky and Luxemburg. Kautsky argues that the party is the precondition of revolutionary action. Luxemburg argues that it is the product of revolutionary mass movement. Lukács finds each view one-sided: "Because it is the party's function to prepare the revolution, it is — simultaneously and equally — both *producer* and *product*, both precondition *and* result of the revolutionary mass movement."[9] The party's role as producer is itself a product of the projected future of proletarian revolution. The party is a product not only of events as they unfold and to which it responds but also of the future that calls it into being, the future that enables it to guides its responses toward it.

Crucial to Lukács's argument is the party's combination of flexibility and consistency. The party has to learn from the struggles of the masses, adjusting its interpretations and practices as necessary. Responses to the present in light of the projected future are inscribed into party structure and theory. Learning from the struggles of the people is possible because of the party's anticipation of the revolution. The party thereby unites the discoveries that arise from the mass struggle with the actuality of the revolution. Belief in revolution arises out of the combination of theory and action: actions appear as revolutionary because the future revolution is calling them into being.

In sum, Lukács presents the actuality of revolution as a projected future. Every decision, every tactic, every compromise anticipates the revolution. To the extent that party practices are coordinated by the future, they both manifest belief in it — as opposed to the more abstract knowledge of revolution posited by social democrats — and help bring it about. Lukács insists that the actuality of revolution distinguishes Lenin's position from both social democrats and left-wing purists. From the perspective of the former, the revolution is always too far off, the proletariat never mature enough, the unions still too weak. From the perspective of the latter, the ripeness of the moment dictates a pure politics, a radical insistence on principles without compromise. Unlike either, the actuality of revolution involves the political time of anticipation and struggle, a time when the future guides the party prepared to usher it in.

REVOLUTION TODAY

In the final volume of their influential trilogy, Hardt and Negri announce: "Revolution is now, finally, becoming the order of the day."[10] Their theory of revolution arises out of an account of the biopolitical character of capitalism in the late twentieth century. Networked communications have transformed the process of production, contributing to its homogenization, decentralization/deterritorialization, and informatization. Knowledge, affect, and communication play a greater role; labor has become "increasingly immaterial."[11] The result is a fundamental change in the relation between production and the reproduction of life: rather than separate from and subordinated to the demands of productive work, "life infuses and dominates all production."[12] With its biopolitical turn, capitalism subsumes the entirety of the social.

On the basis of their analysis of changes in production, Hardt and Negri claim that today "the perspective of revolutionary action has to be conceived on the biopolitical horizon."[13] Such a revolution is a "revolution in life," that is, a revolution that exceeds the range of demands and expectations associated with the labor movement.

Biopolitical revolution has a distinct temporality. In contrast to the projected future provided by the actuality of revolution, revolution today "is no longer imaginable as an event separated from us in the future but has to live in the present, an "exceeding" present that in some sense already contains the future within it."[14] Instead of a future with the capacity to coordinate action in the present, revolution coexists with and within non-revolution. Unable to imagine a future revo-

lution, we cannot use its actuality to decide our tactics. As a distinct
component of political action, tactics falls by the wayside, displaced
by potentials within biopolitical production.

Hardt and Negri imagine revolution as an analogous "kind of
simultaneity," the excess and limit to capitalist command over the
biopolitical production it can never fully capture or control. Biopolitical labor is generally autonomous from capitalist command, emerging out of networked cooperative practices. Capital seeks to capture,
expropriate, and discipline these practices, even as it itself depends on
the creativity that their autonomy unleashes. Bypassing commodifica-
tion, capital extracts value directly from social relations themselves.

Hardt and Negri highlight the democratic dimension of biopolitical labor: the same networked, cooperative structures that
produce the common generate new democratic capacities, and even
"make possible in the political sphere the development of democratic
organizations."[15] For this reason, Hardt and Negri reject "vanguard
organizations." The vanguard party corresponds to a different, earlier,
structure of labor (a different technical composition of the proletariat). According to Hardt's and Negri's periodization, the vanguard
party fits with the early twentieth century's professional factory
workers. The deskilled workers of the mid-twentieth century fit with

*Without a vanguard party, revolutionary potential
can falter. Pictured here, masses demonstrate
in Egypt during the Arab Spring of 2011.*

that period's mass party. The political form appropriate to biopolitical labor, the one appropriate to us now, they argue, must be democratic, cooperative, autonomous and horizontally networked. The vanguard party is inadequate, "anachronistic," because it doesn't look like the networks of contemporary biopolitical production.

This argument is not convincing. Complex networks are not the horizontal, cooperative and autonomous forms that Hardt and Negri imagine. As Albert-Laszlo Barabasi's work on complex networks demonstrates, free choice, growth and preferential attachment produce hierarchies, dramatic differences between the one that is most chosen and preferred and the many that are not.[16] The most popular node or item in a complex network generally has twice as many links as the second most popular, which has more than the third most popular and so, such that there is very little difference among the crowd of those at the bottom but massive differences between top and bottom. This hierarchical structure is pervasive in communicative capitalism. Blockbuster movies, best-selling books, and giant internet hubs like Google, Facebook, YouTube and Baidu all reflect the power law distribution of links in complex networks. The few get a lot; the rest get very little, almost nothing. The idea appears in popular media as the "80/20 rule," the "winner-take-all or winner-take-most character of the economy," and the "long tail" of the many. The ostensibly creative, cooperative and democratic character of networked communication does not eliminate hierarchy. It entrenches hierarchy by using our own choices against us. And, as Barabasi's work on complex networks makes clear, this hierarchy is not imposed from above. It is an immanent effect of free choice, growth and preferential attachment.

A political form mirroring biopolitical production would not be horizontal and democratic. Its democracy would produce power-law distributions, unequal nodes or outcomes, winners and losers, few and many. We see this phenomenon on Twitter as people fight through trending hashtags: hashtags provide common names that serve as loci of struggle. When they trend, they rise above the long tail of the millions of unread, unloved Tweets coursing through the nets. The democratic element — people's choice to use and forward — produces the inequality that lets some hashtags appear as and even be, for a moment, significant. The fact of emergent hierarchies

Occupy Wall Street was a 'leaderless' movement.
Despite its massive reach and support, it was
ultimately undone by concerted state repression.

suggests that an emergent vanguard may well be the political form necessary for struggles under biopolitical conditions.

The structure of the complex networks of biopolitical production indicates that, contra Hardt and Negri, a vanguard party is not anachronistic at all. It is instead a form that corresponds to the dynamics of networked communication. This structure indicates an additional problem with Hardt and Negri's rejection of the vanguard party. They characterize Lenin's party as involving an organizational process that comes from "above" the movements of the multitude. Historically, this insinuation is clearly false. The Bolsheviks were but one group among multiple parties, tendencies and factions acting in the tumultuous context of the Russian Revolution. They were active within the movements of the oppressed workers and peasants. The movements themselves, through victories and defeats, short- and long-term alliances, new forms of cooperation, and advances in political organization gave rise to the party even as the party furthered the movements.

Finally, Hardt and Negri criticize Lenin's party on the grounds of identity. For them, the party is a "new identity," and they think that revolution today must aim at the abolition of identity.[17] Lenin's party is not an identity; it is a process whereby the distinctions of what Hardt and Negri associate with identity are smoothed out and a collective revolutionary will is generated.[18] The party functions through the installation and maintenance of a gap within the field in which identity is given, not as a new identity.

For Hardt and Negri, the goal of revolution is "the generation of new forms of social life."[19] They describe revolutionary struggles as a process of liberation that establishes a common. Such a process, they argue, consolidates insurrection as it institutionalizes new collective habits and practices. Institutions, then, are sites for the management of encounters, extension of social rupture, and transformation of those who compose them.

The resemblance between these institutions and the vanguard party is striking. The party involves a common name, language, and set of tactics. It has practices that establish ways of being together. Its purpose is occupying and extending the gap within society that class struggle denotes. As Lukács insists, Lenin's concept of party organization prioritizes flexibility and consistency; the party has and must have a capacity for self-transformation. What Hardt and Negri describe as the extension of insurrection in an institutional process is another way of theorizing the party.

Because they disavow the party, their version of democratic organization lacks a position that can anticipate the revolution and thereby materialize belief in its actuality. The future does not exercise coordinating capacity. Hardt and Negri emphasize that revolution is "squeezed in the vise between past and future, leaving it very little room for maneuver." They write, "even when revolutionaries think their actions are sufficient to launch us into the future, the past bursts through to reimpose itself." And they conclude, "Revolution's creation of a new form of government holds off the past and opens toward the future."[20] Rather than products of the revolution they produce, revolutionaries in Hardt and Negri's version remain at a distance from the future. Their actions seem disconnected from it, uninformed by it, and hence all the more under the sway of the past. Revolution opens to the future, but a projected future does not call into being the forces that will have produced it.

Lacking a vision of the future capable of orienting action, Hardt and Negri outline instead a platform of demands without a carrier, without a body to fight for them. Their model of institutions suggests that a party or parties could be such a carrier, but rather than presenting their platform as a party platform, Hardt and Negri present them as demands to be made to existing governments and institutions of global governance. The demands are for the provision of basic means of life, global citizenship and access to the commons. They acknowledge that "today's ruling powers unfortunately have no intention of granting even these basic demands."[21] Their response is laughter, "a laugh of creation and joy, anchored solidly in the present."[22] No wonder they do not present their demands as the platform of a party. The demands are not to be fought for. They mark potentials present already in the biopolitical production of the common, limits to capitalist control.

The identification of egalitarian potential in what generally seems a bleak and miserable present is laudable. Absent a party oriented toward its realization, though, it is hard to believe that this potential is stronger than, say, a neo-feudalism of globally connected fortress-cities surrounded by impoverished scavengers competing for access to a better life via networked gaming platforms and desperately defending their last bits of fresh water and arable land from refugees fleeing ever intensifying resource wars while the tiny class of global billionaires eat caviar in gold-plated jets. No practices coordinated by means of the future materialize this belief. Precisely because our setting is one of exploitation, ownership, competition and struggle, our sense of the present has to be tied to the future that results from the realization of some potentials rather than others. The party is the form for this realization insofar as through it the future can produce the actions that will have brought it about.

CONCLUSION

Across the globe, crowds are rupturing the status quo, the actuality of their movement displacing the politics of identity. These mobilized crowds are forcing the Left to return again to questions of organization, endurance, and scale. Having come up against the limits of immediacy and horizontality, activists and organizers alike are thinking again about institutional forms like the party.

Hardt and Negri imply that the party form is outmoded. I have argued that not only do contemporary networks produce power-law distributions of few and many but that emergent hierarchies — particularly when understood in terms of the vanguards and practices that already emerge out of political movement — point to the ways that party organizations emerge. Current examples of this tendency include the adoption of common tactics, names and symbols that bring together previously separate, disparate and even competing struggles. When local and issue politics are connected via a common name, successes in one area advance the struggle as a whole. Separate actions become themselves plus all the others. They instill enthusiasm and inspire imitation.

A global alliance of the radical Left, or, better, a new party of communists, can be knit together from the concentrated forces of already existing groups: militants skilled at direct action, artists adept with symbols and slogans, parties experienced at organizing, issue groups knowledgeable about specific areas of concern, mutual aid networks addressing basic needs. If this new party is to be an agent of revolutionary time, it will have to continue to foster and even amplify the common practices and tactics capable of materializing revolutionary belief. This fostering and amplification requires discipline, choices, conscious planning, and decisions regarding what to prioritize and how to allocate resources and energies. Precisely because of the multiplicity of the experiences of the oppressed, we need the party as the form through which we discipline ourselves, through which we produce the collective political will that will push revolutionary tendencies in an emancipatory egalitarian direction.

Many of us are convinced that capitalist crises have reached a decisive point. We know that the system is fragile, that it produces its own grave-diggers, and that it is held in place by a repressive international state structure. Yet we act as if we did not know this. The party provides a form that can let us believe what we know. □

Endnotes

The October Revolution: workers take power

1   E.H. Carr, "The Bolshevik Revolution 1917-1023,"(London, Palgrave, MacMillan UK, 1950), 1:70-101.

2   V.I. Lenin, "The Tasks of the Proletariat in the Present Revolution," [a.k.a. "The April Theses], Lenin's Collected Works (Moscow: Progress Publishers, 1964), 24:19-26, https://www.marxists.org/archive/lenin/works/1917/apr/04.htm.

3   Carr, "The Bolshevik Revolution," 1:81-82.

4   V.I. Lenin, "From a Publicist's Diary (Peasants and Workers)," Lenin's Collected Works (Moscow: Progress Publishers, 1977), 25:278-286, https://www.marxists.org/archive/lenin/works/1917/sep/11.htm.

5   V.I. Lenin, "Meeting of the Petrograd Soviet of Workers' and Soldiers' Deputies," Lenin's Collected Works, 4th ed. (Moscow: Progress Publishers, 1964), 26:239-41.

Why we continue to defend the Soviet Union

1   Mark Fields, "Health personnel in the Soviet Union: achievements and problems," American Journal of Public Health 56, no. 11 (1966): 1904-1920.

The role of leadership in revolutionary struggle

1.   Letter from Afar, March 12, 1917

Socialism and the legacy of the Soviet Union

1   1918 Constitution of the Russian Socialist Federated Soviet Republic, Chapter 2, Article 3. https://www.marxists.org/history/ussr/government/constitution/1918/article1.htm

2   1918 Constitution, Chapter 2, Article 3, point c. https://www.
    marxists.org/history/ussr/government/constitution/1918/arti-
    cle1.htm
3   1918 Constitution, Chapter 2, Article 3, point g. https://www.marx-
    ists.org/history/ussr/government/constitution/1918/article1.htm

Lenin, World War I and the social roots of opportunism
1   V.I Lenin, "Imperialism, the Highest Stage of Capitalism."
    Selected Works, International Publishers, 1971, p. 261.
2   Lenin, "The Discussion on Self-Determination Summed Up."
    Collected Works (1972), vol. 22, p. 343.
3   V.I. Lenin, "Imperialism," p. 125
4   Lenin, "The International Socialist Congress in Stuttgart."
    Collected Works (1972), vol. 13, p. 77.
5   V.I Lenin, "Congress in Stuttgart"
6   Lenin, "Imperialism and the Split in Socialism." Collected Works
    (1972), vol. 23, p. 107.

Lenin and the right of nations to self-determination
1   Karl Marx, "Capital," (Moscow: Progress Publishers, 1965), https://
    www.marxists.org/archive/marx/works/1867-c1/index.htm.
2   "The Right of Nations to Self-determination," 1914
3   "The Question of Nationalities or 'Autonomisation,'" Collected
    Works v.36, Progress Publishers, 1971, p.607
4   "Draft program for the fourth congress of social-democrats of
    the Latvian area," May 1913
5   "Theses on the national question," June 1913

Nadezhda Krupskaya
1   Quotations from the works of Nadezhda Konstantinova
    Krupskaya are taken from Pedagogiceskie socienenija, Vol. 9,
    pg 226, [Educational Works in Eleven Volumes], Moscow, APN
    RSFSR, 1957-63.

Black Bolsheviks and white lies
    References
    Hughes, Langston. (1984). I wonder as I wander: An autobi-
ographical journey . New York: Hill and Wang.

Robeson, Paul. (1978). Paul Robeson speaks: Writings, speeches, interviews 1918-1974, ed. by P.S. Foner. New York: Citadel.

1   Claude McKay, "The Negro and Radical Thought," The Crisis," 22, no.3 (1921): 102.
2   James, "Holding Aloft the Banner of Ethiopia," 165.
3   Langston Hughes, "Ballads of Lenin," vol. 1 of The Collected Works of Langston Hughes, ed. Arnold Rampersad (Columbia: University of Missouri Press, 2001), 140.
4   Langston Hughes, "I Wonder as I Wander," vol. 14 of The Collected Works of Langston Hughes, ed. Arnold Rampersad (Columbia: University of Missouri Press, 2001), 104.
5   Hughes, "I Wonder as I Wander," 98.
6   Hughes, "I Wonder as I Wander," 98.
7   Hughes, "I Wonder as I Wander," 104.
8   Hughes, "I Wonder as I Wander," 111.
9   Hughes, "I Wonder as I Wander," 116.
10 W.E.B. Du Bois, "The Quest for the Abolition of the Color Line." In Studies in African American History and Culture by Zhang Juguo, edited by Graham Russell Hodges, 138. New York: Routledge, 2001.

How the ideas of 'The State and Revolution' changed history

1   Known as the Great October Socialist Revolution, started with a two-day insurrection on 25 October 1917 (by the Julian or Old Style calendar, which corresponds to 7 November 1917 in the Gregorian or New Style calendar).
2   Lenin, "The State and Revolution," p. 6
3   Sawer, Marian, The Genesis of State and Revolution, p. 215, 216, The Socialist Register, 1977, ed. Ralph Millibrand and John Saville
4   Nickolai Bukharin, submitted an essay; Towards a Theory of the Imperialist State in July 1916 for a series edited by Lenin, who rejected it for publication on the basis that it was erroneous. Bukharin published another version of the article in December 1916 under the title The Imperialist Pirate State.
5   Sawer, "The Genesis of State and Revolution," p. 217
6   Lenin, "The State and Revolution," p. 5
7   Lenin, "The State and Revolution," p. 32, Marx, Karl, The Eighteenth Brumaire of Louis Bonaparte

8   Letter to Joseph Weydemeyer
9   Marx and Engels, 1872 Preface to the German Edition of "The Communist Manifesto," p. 2, Struik, Dirk "Birth of the Communist Manifesto," p. 130, New World Paperbacks
10 Riazanov, David, Karl Marx and Fredrich Engels, An Introduction to Their Lives and Work, p. 198, Monthly Review
11 Ibid, p. 218
12 Sawer, "The Genesis of State and Revolution," p. 211
13 Nettle, Peter, "The German Social Democratic Party 1890-1914 As a Political Model, p. 78 Past and Present, No. 30, April 1965
14 Ibid
15 Becker and Majidi, "Socialists and War," appendix p. 41, Manifesto of the International Socialist Congress
16 Ibid, p. 46
17 Lenin, What Has the Trial of the Russian Social-Democratic Faction Proved?
18 Sawer, "The Genesis of State and Revolution," p. 212
19 Ibid, p. 211
20 Ibid, p. 216
21 Ibid, p. 4
22 Lenin, The Russian Revolution and the Tasks of the Workers of All Countries, March 12/25, 1917
23 Lenin, The April Theses, April 4, 1917
24 Lenin, "Several Theses," Sotsial-Demokrat No. 47, October 13, 1915
25 Ibid, Point 2
26 Evans, Alfred B., "Rereading Lenin's State and Revolution," p. 4 Slavic Review, Spring 1987, Vol. 46, No. 1
27 Lenin, The April Theses
28 Lenin, Meeting Of The Petrograd Soviet Of Workers' And Soldiers' Deputies, October 25 (November 7), 1917

The actuality of revolution

1   Jean-Pierre Dupuy, Economy and the Future, trans. M.B. DeBevoise, East Lansing, MI: Michigan State University Press, 2014, 110.
2   Dupuy, 116.
3   Projected future thus functions differently from the program put

forth by Nick Srnicek and Alex Williams in Inventing the Future, London, Verso, 2015.

4 Dupuy, 129.
5 Lukács, 12.
6 Ibid. (italics in original)
7 Lukács, 30.
8 Lukács, 29.
9 Lukács, 32.
10 Michael Hardt and Antonio Negri, Commonwealth, Cambridge, MA: The Belknap Press of Harvard University Press, 2009, 344.
11 Michael Hardt and Antonio Negri, Empire, Cambridge, MA, Harvard University Press, 2000, Empire 365.
12 Hardt and Negri, Empire, 365.
13 Commonwealth, 239.
14 Commonwealth, 242-243.
15 Commonwealth, 354.
16 See my discussion in Crowds and Party, London, Verso, 2016, 12-13.
17 Commonwealth, 334.
18 As Lukács writes in "Towards a Methodology of the Problem of Organization," "the Communist Party as the revolutionary form of consciousness of the proletariat is a process by nature," 316, italics in original; and, "the party exists in order to hasten the process by which these distinctions are smoothed out," 326 — the distinctions Lukács is referring to are stratifications within the class.
19 Commonwealth, 354.
20 Commonwealth, 360.
21 Commonwealth, 382.
22 Commonwealth, 383.

Don't fight alone – Join a revolutionary organization!

JOIN the PSL

The Party for Socialism and Liberation is comprised of leaders and activists, workers and students, of all backgrounds. Organized in branches across the country, the PSL brings together a new generation of revolutionaries alongside veterans of the people's movements with decades of experience.

The PSL is involved in a wide range of struggles, from local battles over affordable housing and racist police brutality, to the fight for a higher minimum wage and union rights, to the global issues of imperialist war and environmental destruction.

We are united in our belief that capitalism – the system in which all wealth and power is held by a tiny group of billionaires and their state – is the source of the main problems confronting humanity today.

It must be replaced by socialism, a system where poor and working people have power, and the wealth of society is used in a planned and sustainable way to meet people's needs.

Our mission is to link the everyday struggles of oppressed and exploited people to the fight for a new world.

Join us!

Contact us at
PSLweb.org/contact

Made in the USA
Monee, IL
20 May 2024

58681030R10095